FULL
FRONTAL
STUPIDITY

Barry Parham

also by
BARRY PARHAM

Why I Hate Straws
An offbeat worldview of an offbeat world

Sorry, We Can't Use Funny

Blush
Politics and other unnatural acts

The Middle-Age of Aquarius

WHAT READERS ARE SAYING
ABOUT THE AUTHOR
and

FULL FRONTAL
STUPIDITY

"…delights, amuses, and is laugh-out-loud funny…"

"relentless, biting, intelligent…Parham's best yet!"

"unique…versatile…hilarious"

"Political Correctness takes a beating when Parham's pen is in hand"

"a masterpiece of wit, satire and curmudgeonly humor"

"Why isn't somebody monitoring this man's medication?"

DEDICATION

To remembered friends

Fast, Em & Thea, Sullivan Susie, Clan Coleman, Clan Cheezem,
Spike, Seamus & Panera Mike (sour cream cheese, please), Fish,
Tim (& Morgan), HighPockets, Slats, Nipper, Caj, AmSa, Jo
Beanie, Red One-Seven, Chuck (or Charles, but never Charlie),
Coach, the other Coach, my Other Brother,
and Amy Mac

You know who you are.

Thanks for it all.

Table of Nonsense

FIVEWORD

Well, here we are. Book Number Five. And I still haven't heard from Oprah.

I try not to dwell on that.

People are always coming up to me and asking, "How did you do it? How did you become such a wildly successful humor writer in spite of having serious ferret issues without ever getting endorsed by Oprah's must-read list, 'Books My Driver Said Somebody Said Somebody Heard Somebody's Aunt Said Somebody Liked'?"

And that leads to the inevitable, awkward moment - I have to point out to these celebrity chasers that they've (understandably) confused me with someone else; some household hearth god like Brad Pitt, or Lindsay Lohan, or Cplnoxtpotl (Oprah's driver).

After that, the star-seekers generally mumble their excuses and head back to their own lane at the bowling alley.

But I can't help noticing that Lindsay Lohan's progressive parade of mug shots are beginning to look more and more like me.

I try not to dwell on that.

Simple Misdemeanor
Stupid (Social Media)

~*~*~

"Ignorance is a vast darkness we all shine in."

Virgil

~*~*~*~*~

Full Frontal Stupidity

Knock, Knock

(Some people take humor way too seriously)

A few days ago, while watching the news, I stopped watching the news.

The news victim of the hour was current candidate (and ex-business non-failure) Herman Cain, and the on-duty network Hair Helmets were presenting a studied, bipartisan analysis of Cain's views on Keynesian economic macro-adjustments as they might adversely affect America's frontier-free foreign policy.

Right.

Actually, the topic was how many mammals Cain might have hit on during his long career of doing no such thing, while being staggeringly successful without whining. I lost count (and interest) when the list of sexual victims grew to include Rick Perry, and, on a separate occasion, Perry's hair.

Enough, already.

So I flicked the remote, turned off the TV, and then spent some time reading a fascinating scientific article on the evolutionary origins of humor. I learned three things:

1) Humor, like sexual repression, has been around for a long time, and both are pretty funny.
2) Sexual repression is the underlying cause of just about all bad behavior exhibited in humans, lab rats, and politicians.
3) Some people have a thesaurus that's *way* better than mine.

The article was written by two professional synonym-wranglers at some university in northern Manitoba, that internationally recognized hotbed of hilarity. I think the general thrust of their article was that humor has evolved over the last 6 million years, and if they're going with 'evolved,' they obviously wrote the piece without watching much prime time TV.

I have to say that I challenge their thesis. Personally, I'm not convinced that humor has evolved very much at all, as evidenced by a recently discovered glyph of the first three jokes ever told:

1) Two hominids knuckle-walked into a bar...
2) Take my hunter-gatherer. Please!
3) Knock.

(Source: Jurassic Journal of Comic Bas-Relief, 1 April MCXIV BC)

So I'm fairly certain that the article was really just a contrived vehicle to let the authors show off a bunch of big words, probably hoping to impress chicks in Manitoban single-hunter-gatherer bars (assuming Manitoba has sexual repression). I can't think of any other reason for otherwise normal people to deliberately employ silly, made-up words like 'exapted,' 'phylogenetic conspecifics,' and 'Schopenhauer.'

Really? Exapted? Please. 'Exapted' sounds like some kind of galactic disciplinary action - like big green alien parents taking away ET's ray gun.

"EXTRA WILSON TERRESTRIAL!"
(You know you're in trouble when your parents use your full name. Even in outer space.)
"Nzxtmk?"
"Don't nzxtmk me, young man! You ate Elliott, didn't you? You are *so* exapted! Just wait till your Y-Chromosome donor phones home! Keep it up, young hominid - I'll turn this spaceship right around!"

But simply saying 'exapted' and 'quasi-syntactical recursion' with a straight face wasn't enough for these guys in Manitoba. Not by half. The next time you single guys corner a colleen and are struggling for that just-right ice-breaker, try this crowd-pleaser:

You: "You know, ontogeny can sometimes recapitulate phylogeny."
Woman You Are So Never Gonna See Again: "Weird. I was just thinking that very same thing."
You, Anyway: "Wanna go to my place and see my glyph?"

The authors' exhaustive source materials on humor even included quasi-exapted observations from Charles Darwin. You'll remember Mr. Darwin as that 19th Century botanist who was hired to sail around the world looking for examples of Darwinism; instead, however, the shameless little shirker got sidetracked while watching a Galapagos finch trying to suck food through a stick, after which Darwin concluded that a humongous tortoise would eventually evolve into filmmaker Michael Moore. Or maybe it was the other way around.

Darwin also proposed a concept he called 'natural selection,' a theory which attempted to describe the complex inner workings of seemingly chaotic systems, like nation-states, and the NFL draft. Darwin conjectured that nature selected evolutionary winners (and culled losers) based on superior qualities, which still doesn't explain Michael Moore. Darwin referred to this phenomenon as 'survival of the fittest,' a proposition that was soon debunked in favor of the more obvious explanation, 'survival of the most-heavily armed.'

Obviously, by this point in his voyage, Darwin had ... how can I put it gently? ... Darwin had popped his clutch. Perhaps due to scurvy, perhaps due to spending way too much time observing giant turtles in equatorial singles bars, Darwin was clearly out of control. As our Manitoban friends point out, Darwin even managed to link evolutionary survival tactics to tickling.

Tickling, as a survival tactic. This may be the best evidence to date that Darwin not only studied interesting plants - he also knew something about interesting brownies, if you catch my drift.

Darwin noticed that the places we tickle each other - the throat, the belly, the soles of our feet - are also the places most vulnerable to attack from predators. So Darwin assumed that this was Uncle Evo at work again, subtly teaching us how to protect those vulnerable spots. This is obviously a stretch; if this theory were true, we'd all be wearing shoes on our neck.

By the way - this deep fascination Darwin had for survival issues is what psychiatrists call an 'obsession,' what politicians call an 'agenda,' and what students call 'is this gonna be on the exam?'

My own 'evolutionary laughter' theory is much simpler: Only mammals can laugh, because only mammals have milk, which is biologically required if you hear a joke so funny that milk spurts out of your nose.

And, if I might, may I humbly point out that Charles Darwin apparently never noticed this vital nose-to-lactose corollary.

Of course, some will take exception to my 'mammals only' argument, claiming that if grocers can sell soy milk, then soy must be a mammal. This is a classic example of what psychiatrists call 'projecting conspecific transference' and what I call 'being rock stupid.' In response, I'll gently remind that there's just not a great deal of 'soy' humor, now, is there?

"Two tasteless meat substitutes walked into a salad bar..."

But, lest you think our semi-frozen scholars got all that grant money just to talk about tickling, let's quickly riffle through some of their other observations - opinions about evolution, humor, and why rats giggle.

Witness:

"During conversations with each other, women laugh 126% more than men ... and it has been observed that persons in higher positions of authority laugh less often."
The takeaway here is simple: if your boss is a man, and you like your job, shut your smart mouth.

"Theory-of-mind researchers have shown that children under age 6 have a particularly difficult time distinguishing lies from jokes."
As do sociopaths, and news anchors at MSNBC.

"Activation in the medial ventral prefrontal cortex bilaterally correlates with how funny the joke is."
Great. Now they tell me. And all this time I've been watching to see if anybody slaps their knee.

"Scientists detected a 50kHz chirp in young rats during social interactions resembling play, and wondered if this positive affective vocalization could be related to human laughter."
That's just sad.

Think about that. One day, in some lab somewhere, some over-zealous undergrad shouted, "Look! The rats are demonstrating play-like behavior during a social interaction again!"

But it's a cautionary tale, isn't it? I suppose that's the evolutionary price we all pay for leaving young, impressionable turtles alone with Michael Moore.

Full Frontal Stupidity

Can You Borrow *What?*

(If this is the American dream, please wake me up.)

Ah. Saturday morning in suburban America. The sounds, the smells. The camaraderie, the cable outages, the collapsing property values. Backyard barbecue served here, custody papers served there. The endless parade of roof replacement scam squads. The bank-dodging "everything must go" yard sales, the revolving army of moving vans. The lazy flutter of foreclosure notices.

I live in a nice, middle-class neighborhood. "Neighborhood" is a complex Old English term, roughly translated as "ye olde credit default swappe." (Call Ethelred today for ye very own! Verily, canst this offer not last!)

My neighborhood is one of those planned communities with a cute, oxymoronic name, like Nepalese Shores, or Aerie Caverns, or Upside Downs. The developer followed the standard Bulldoze-Claw-Cajole plan: sell off every extant tree, scrape off every micron of topsoil, buy off every minor official. Nudge-

11

nudge-wink-wink your way past your ex-wife's second cousin at the Building Inspector's office, slap up several hundred mildly divergent versions of six pre-fab floor plans, disconnect your "Award-Winning Service - After The Sale!" phone number and then vanish from the known universe.

In my cute, oxymoronic neighborhood, Mordor Shires (Third Age, Phase Two), I live at the end of a cul-de-sac. "Cul-de-sac" is a complex French term, roughly translated as "Hey, Joe, see if you can't shoehorn one more 3BR Portsmouth Deluxe in there, in-between the *legal* plats. Wink-wink."

Now, in and of itself, living on the toe of a cul-de-sac is pretty cool. Zoning variances allow me an oversized back yard and, in the evenings, oncoming headlights keep my daylilies nervous, wondering if today is *The Day*. Plus, when the developer's mop-up team got around to the house numbering scheme, they got confused. As a result, my house is number 26, but the house on my left is #24 and the house on my right is #25. So I'm constantly getting to read other people's mail. (After all, there's a *reason* the US Post Office lost 8.5 billion dollars in 2010.)

However, in my case, there's a down side to living at the end of the block. Due to prevailing wind patterns, my cul-de-sac acts as some sort of telescoping wind tunnel, focusing and funneling anything that is loose, or gets loose, or loses its footing, down the street and into my yard, particularly if it's something that's brightly colored, non-biodegradable and/or marginally toxic.

SIDEBAR: I was going to say that the wind blows things down the street and "onto my lawn," but honesty compels me. I don't own a lawn - I have a yard. A yard is that buffer zone that surrounds your physical dwelling and ends at your neighbor's buffer zone, usually demarked by a disputed fence that leans like bad teeth and a half-dead tree that has even less dependable roots than the teeth. A lawn, on the other hand, implies commitment, which immediately rules me out. The term suggests that the owner cares about his "yard" enough to treat it as a "lawn," even during the heat of August in the American South, a sadistic chunk of the calendar when small, furry forest animals have been known to suddenly explode, or at least ask to.)

So, I'm forever staring out my window (literal translation: "working from home") as stuff blows at, against, and past my house.

And does stuff ever blow! Mail, garbage, laundry, lunch wrappers. Foreclosure threats and savings account invites, often from the same bank. "Vote For Me, Please" pleas; vast savings on volume discounts; very small pets. Realtor placards with "For Sale" scribbled out and "For Rent" Sharpied in, or appended with "NU LO PRICE!" (spelled, apparently, by someone with a Master's degree in Post Office)

Mind you, not all of this wind-mailed detritus is necessarily a bad thing. When the local pizza delivery franchise issues a new discount coupon, for instance, I end up with dozens. As a single guy, I'm set for weeks. The same goes for our four nearby Chinese takeaways; Great Wall Joy Food, Panda Food Joy Wall, Wall of Great Panda Joy, and Bank of America.

But the rest are mostly Mom-n-Pop entities offering unique products or niche services, like low-maintenance vinyl siding treatments ("now in creative geometricalized patternizations!"), miniaturized rock-garden river rapids ("tiny inbred banjo player, not included"), or ferret whispering.

And, interestingly, some of these marketers have taken clever steps to ensure that rogue wind gusts don't defeat their advertising efforts. For example, they'll slip their little flyer in a small Ziploc bag and then shovel in a short handful of pebbles or pea gravel - the idea being that the rocks' extra weight will keep the wind from carrying off their bulk-printed two-color advertisements, touting custom-treated balsa decks or free-range parrot colon cleansing.

Fortunately, these bag-lobbing advertisers usually include their *own* home address somewhere inside the rock-filled bag they toss, uninvited, onto my property, making it quite easy for someone like me to figure out where *they* live, sometime around two in the morning, if you get my drift.

Anyway, here's what went down this week at #26 Mordor Shires. I was out in my "lawn," collecting several hundred wind-whipped yellow flyers advertising the services of Mark, The Lakeland Area's Undisputed Mulch King. ("Because Compost Happens!")

A few more-or-less consecutive house numbers up, I noticed a U-Haul truck in a driveway. So I watched for a while to see if they were taking stuff out of the truck, or putting stuff in; to see if I was gaining, or losing, a neighbor. But I never saw anybody, doing anything, period.

Maybe they'd simply decided to buy a U-Haul truck.

And then a friend told me about a story she'd heard on the news: apparently, some people were renting moving vans and using them as temporary meth labs.

Ah, well. At least *somebody's* working in America. And if there's a market out there, clamoring for temporary meth, who am I to tsk-tsk, eh?

A little while later, while I was loading pea gravel in the scatter-gun (if you get my drift), there came a knock on my door. Lo and behold, it was my neighbors from the U-Haul house! A slimmish young couple, obviously on a first-name basis with several tattoo parlors, they asked if they might borrow a cup of sugar and, if it wasn't a huge bother, maybe some anhydrous ammonia or phenylpropanolamine, and a dash or two of red phosphorus.

Now, I like to be a helpful neighbor. And I had no immediate need for that occasionally handy keg of phenyl in the basement, nor the red phosphorus I keep in the fridge door for Jehovah's Witness counter-measures, but *please* ... processed sugar? I haven't used processed sugar in *decades*.

But, to be honest ... well, *yeah!* What do *you* think? Of *course* I wondered what they were up to! Of *course* I got nervous!

What if these two were miscreants who hadn't acquired the proper permits? What if they were simply enabling parents of impressionable children, gearing up to...

(gasp)

sell lemonade without a license?

Trousers 2.0

(From fabric to Facebook. Sometimes progress isn't.)

I finally bought a new laptop (a *computer*, not an abdomen). And everything went just fine until I got cocky and tried to use it (not the abdomen, the computer).

I remember the first time I saw it (the computer). It beckoned to me from an online ad. It was thin, fast, smart, tactile, responsive, and had a mute button - half of me wanted to buy it, the other half wanted to date it. It was awesome, or sweet, or all that, or def, or non-epic fail, or the shizzle, or whatever phrase we're using this week to represent the concept "good." It was love at first sight, albeit a very sick, virtual, Oedipal, man-attracted-to-motherboard kind of love.

Until recently, I'd been immune to the urge to upgrade laptops. After all, I don't play graphics-intensive games where the goal is to create graphic intensive-care victims. I don't travel, I'm not an online social media junkie, and when I hear "algorithm," I think oxymoron. (Al Gore doesn't *have* rhythm.) Plus, my credit rating hovers somewhere between "house pet" and "Greece."

See, I was entirely happy with my "old" laptop. It lets me type, though it doesn't care much for my way cool grammar shizzle, or my speling, or my, like, literary style and stuff. It occasionally lets me win at Solitaire (but not Scrabble). It correctly performs complex mathematical calculations for me, as far as I know. It lets me drag colorful rectangles and circles from one place on the screen to another until they're perfectly left-aligned, a disturbingly comforting exercise, I'll admit, though completely useless from a business or social perspective.

Best of all, it lets me put it in my car and take it places, so I can be "working remotely" from anywhere. "Working remotely" is a complicated tax concept that essentially describes the act of paying exceptionally manipulative people to *stay home and not work*. "Working remotely" translates, roughly, as "not even remotely working."

Historical Sidebar: Members of Congress refer to this handy little "money for nothing" trick as "getting to know our constituents."

But, like many things in the life of someone who builds websites for a living, the "computer upgrade" decision wasn't really up to me. Since I build websites for a living, I am effectively under the control of a global mega-power who, for legal reasons, I'll refer to as MicroSauce. MicroSauce is an American company that makes software updates. That's it. That's their whole job - to release updates, version upgrades, and something called Service Packs.

(MicroSauce never says "bug fix." They say "Service Pack." And when you call them for support, they never say "Hello." They say "I am having one or more help deskness for getting your MicroSauce to bliss." I don't know why that is. But half of me wants to date it.)

Now, I suppose that, if your entire corporate strategy is to sell updates to stuff, you have to figure out ways to keep updating stuff. And MicroSauce is very, very good at updating stuff. On any given day, they may release ten, fifteen updates, sometimes for stuff made by other companies, including food. Sometimes they'll release an update to stuff that you're updating, *while you're updating it*, generating a system overload guaranteed to turn any defenseless computer into a whimpering idiot, reminiscent of James Mason during the closing scenes from "Lolita." (Note: this may result in what is known as a "dual boot," which is when you kick your computer off the back deck, then run down the deck steps so you can kick it again.)

But the real genius behind MicroSauce is their notorious ability to release software updates that condescendingly snort at your computer's hardware. No matter what kind of pumped PC you own, it's never enough for the next MicroSauce upgrade. It's uncanny. Somehow, they find out. Somehow, they know.

(MicroSauce is also notorious for releasing upgrades that contain confusing messages like this: *To finish, click 'Continue.'* Pardon me? If I have to continue, then we're not really finished yet, are we, Rinpoche?)

And since the cool tools I use to build websites are made by MicroSauce, I have to follow their cool tool rules. I have to comply with their "hardware requirements." And so, recently, when MicroSauce released the latest updated Service Pack to upgrade my Service Pack's upgraded update, my old computer simply could no longer keep up with the cyber-Joneses.

So, as they say in the hive-mind of the Star Trek Borg collective, and in the IRS, "Resistance is futile." I had to upgrade my "ancient" computer.

According to the internet, the first computing device was something called the Jacquard Loom, an amazing device invented in 1801 by a European man named Joseph Loom.

Historical Sidebar: Joseph's middle name was "Marie," but apparently that happens a lot in Europe.

The Jacquard Loom was a relatively primitive device which, like my old computer, didn't support RAM upgrades or federally-funded condom distribution in kindergartens. (On the other hand, my computer can't make a quilt.) But what this revolutionary new loom *did* do was use punch cards to control individual warp yarns. Prior to this breakthrough, I suppose, gangs of rogue warp yarns just roamed the streets of Europe, sleeping in parks, holding up misspelled signs and demanding that corporations stop making all those nasty profits. I suppose Medieval tailors were forever running about, trying to manage great thundering herds of warp yarns, a futile effort which led directly to the invention of nudity.

Historical Sidebar: Ultimately, of course, warp yarns faced total extinction, along with dodos, dinosaurs, and Henry VIII's wives. The last extant warp was memorialized in "The Warp of 1812," a famous symphonic fresco by Charles Marie Dickens.

As it turned out, Madame or Monsieur Jacquard had not really invented the punch card system at all. He or she had only improved on an earlier invention, dreamed up around 1745 by one Jacques de Vaucanson, a flash-in-the-pan citizen immortalized by his coinage of the term "binary" (literal translation: "having two naries"). It was a very simple system: a hole meant Yes, no hole meant No. This system still works today, except in southern Florida elections.

But Joseph or Marie was a man or woman of action, and they collectively contacted a Vatican "fixer" named Tony the Nose, a campaign bundler who had a penchant for conflict resolution and a gift for negotiation. And a boat.

And the rest is history. The punch card-based machinery in the factories of Jacquard Loom, Inc., allowed an "ordinary" workman to produce the most beautiful patterns, quickly and consistently. It was an overnight success. Soon, people all over Europe were not naked, mostly.

But before Joseph Marie's wife, Harold, could invent insider trading and file for an IPO, the plant had to shut down, because France was not a right-to-work etat.

Historical Sidebar: Many years later, another pre-computer innovator, Charles "Warp" Babbage, used the punch card idea to store programs in his "Analytical engine," which he named after his goldfish, Google. And Google, of course, led to the internet, which was invented by Al Gore, driven into a ditch by George W. Bush, and miraculously saved by Barack Obama.

Full Frontal Stupidity

(It's sad when the review's better than the movie.)

Looking for something to do next weekend? Well, you could rent a movie I just watched about the Norse god, Thor. Or you could just spend ninety minutes hitting yourself in the head with a brick.

Either way, you'll be guilty of murder. Either way, you'll have butchered an hour and a half.

Imagine this:

"I'm Thor."
"You are?"
"Yeth. I'm really thor. My arm hurth."

You think *that's* lame? Wait till you hear the *real* script.

As we all know from our in-depth undergraduate cross-doctrinal studies in ancient Scandinavian theologies, or from comic books,

Full Frontal Stupidity

Thor is a hunky, cut-through-the-chitchat-and-get-down-to-business-type god, with blonde hair and a blunt hammer, who hails from Sweden or somewhere like that. (I could be wrong about Sweden, but as an undergraduate, I missed the day when they pulled out a map and pointed to Scandinia.)

Now, before I start getting e-hate mail from the Norse Deity Pantheon Anti-Defamation League (and I'm quite sure there is one), let me say that I was a big fan of comic book Thor. That Thor was this great big football hero-looking guy with long blonde hair, and he could use words like "Thee" and "Thy" without getting called a weenie by his junior high school peer group.

But comic book Thor was nowhere to be found in this movie. This Thor spent most of his on-camera face time whining and saying "No." No matter what kind of good advice he'd get from his deity peer group, movie Thor would pout and refuse to listen. He just jogged back and forth, from mystical dimension to mystical dimension, along with a nearly dressed deity named Breastus Maximus.

In the entire movie, I don't think Thor ever said "Thee" once, but it was hard to tell, what with all the whining. And all the Breastus Maximus.

By the way, Breastus Maximus was not her real name. According to the internet, Thor's distaff playmate was a ridiculously over-mascara'd Valhallan named Jarnsaxa (literal translation: Gladys Knight, but with Gothic eyeliner).

And movie Thor didn't even have long blonde hair! He looked like a surfer with chin stubble and questionable dental hygiene. I kept waiting for him to hop in a hopped-up '69 Dodge Charger and start running moonshine with his brother, Luke Duke.

Somehow, the movie's "Historical Accuracy" department decided that all the good deities in Valhalla used to wear the same outfit - some minimal undergarment, practically no pants at all, and a 250-pound wooly mammoth fur coat. But they all wore monstrous leather-laced leggings, perhaps because they wore no pants. The leggings looked like paint rollers look after being soaked in water. Everybody looked like they were on their way to some mystical Aesir Aerobics class.

Given this movie's extremely high Lame Quotient, it wouldn't be right for me to use the word "plot," so let's just discuss some of the scenes. Witness:

- Odin, the immortal god of Valhalla, either gets killed or gets hidden somewhere by that evil prankster Loki, the god of Stupid Pet Tricks And Congressional Ethics. (I know, I know. Odin, the immortal god. Apparently, in Scandinia, you can be immortal *and* dead.) In the movie, Loki looks like Fleetwood Mac's Lindsay Buckingham, but with a bad skin condition.
- Odin's disembodied voice commands Breastus Maximus to protect young Thor until he grows up, or the universe ends, whichever comes first.
- Breastus collects Thor, who asks, "Where are we going?" Breastus replies, "To my dwelling." See? See what I mean about the script?

- (Author's note: "Dwelling" is one of those words that nobody has *ever* used in an actual out-loud conversation on this planet. *Never.* It's like "persnickety," or "Congressional ethics.")

- Somehow, perhaps due to Norse deity insider trading, Loki manages to acquire Thor's hammer, a magical weapon of mass destruction that, to be honest, looks like a concrete block popsicle.

- Thor and Breastus spend the next eighty-one minutes trying to find Loki, Thor's hammer, and the plot.

- Loki, equally confused about what movie he's in, unleashes three giant dogs with Egyptian heads and tattooed chests. He and the giant mythical tattooed dogs roam around Los Angeles, which surprises no one.

- Suddenly, Breastus and Thor materialize through a magic portal. They take a moment to consult one of those fold-up gas station road maps, despite the fact that they're immortals with access to magic portals. Since they're in LA, she teaches Thor how to use a semi-automatic weapon.

- (Author's note: It was at this point in the movie when I started looking for a brick.)

- Loki manages to find Thor by smelling the pavement. I am not good enough to make this stuff up.

- At this point, Thor shows up with two swords, because the movie's producers forgot to hire a Continuity department. Next, naturally, Thor strips down to his chain mail Underalls and performs that same, tired, nun-chuck-like, two-sword-swishy-crossy maneuver that all movie barbarians are forced by law to do at least once per movie. After the obligatory scimitar-swinging, Thor marries a Kennedy and runs for Governor of California.

- It begins to rain, in a film noir slow-motion kind of way. Somehow, Thor finds himself in a cave (see "Continuity department, lack of"). Inside the dark cave are three magic whispering people called The Norns (literal translation: Gladys Knight's Original Backup Singers). Nothing much happens, which apparently is the theme of this movie.

- Breastus appears from somewhere (see "Script, lack of"), and she and Thor try to find their way out of the Norn cave. Shortly, she finds a wall. Breastus says, "Can you feel anything?" Thor - the hero of millions of young boys, the immortal God of Thunder - replies, "A wall."

- I am not good enough to make this stuff up.

- Meanwhile, in an entirely different movie, Loki unleashes a new dreadnought from his eternal arsenal of mystical, immortal weapons - a bone. A magic bone.

- Yeth. A *bone*, for Odin's sake.

- Thor, energized by having added "wall" to his vocabulary, reappears in LA and hits Loki. Loki drops his magic bone, because Thor hit him. Next, in a line sure to trigger the keen radar of every Academy Award "Best Screenplay" judge, Loki says, "Give me back the bone."

- Not to be outdone by Loki sniffing sidewalks, Thor talks to the bone.

- Oh, no, he didn't!

- Oh, yeth, he did.

- Breastus Maximus did not appear in this pivotal bone-talking scene, because her West Coast agent had landed her a last-minute gig as a guest-god on "Dancing With The Netherworld Stars." But she did show up just as Thor was shaking the magic bone, as if the sculpted, immortal moron thought that jiggling it would make the bone speak up. She posed in profile and managed not to look condescending.

- (Author's note: At this point, it's entirely possible that I hit a Derision Overload and passed out.)

- Suddenly, both Thor and Loki realize that there are only five minutes left in the movie. So, naturally, they start fighting, because they're guys. Thor seems to have misplaced his semi-automatic street gun, but somehow he got his hammer back, possibly thanks to some nebulous Hammer Deity government bailout. Thor hurls the hammer at Loki, but Loki deflects the blow, and the hammer kills two warehouse walls and a commuter bus. Thor pouts, reloads and swings again, but Loki sprays Thor dead in the face with a handful of something - either magic dust, or crack. (after all, they *are* in LA)

- Fortunately for mankind, Loki trips over the closing credits. Thor closes in and goes all Mallet Monster on him, which is not going to help Loki's skin condition.

- As Loki lay dying, in an immortal, can't-really-die kind of way, Breastus appears through a nearby magic portal and poses in profile. Thor tries to hit on her, because he's a guy. Breastus, however, shuns Thor and reveals her secret - she is, in fact, a he. Breastus is a former football coach, disguised and hiding out in Valhalla, until things settle down at Penn State.

Have a great weekend! Let me know if you want to borrow my brick.

Full Frontal Stupidity

Skirts v. Skins

(Men are from Mars. Now they're here. That's what can happen when you won't ask for directions.)

As an adult (sic), one discovery I keep making, over and over, is that most of what they taught us as kids in school is bunk. Reams of facts with a Real World Reusability Factor of zero. I don't know about you, but in my social circles, the per capita income of pre-industrial Europe almost never comes up.

Not once in all my years have I ever been asked, "What, again, is the Latin third person plural form of the verb 'to love'?" I've never had to face a social pre-qualification that began with, "Okay, I'll go out with you, but only after you discuss, in 250 words or less, the broad use of irony in the short stories of O. Henry. Include examples."

For over half a century now, I've been avoiding responsibility, and salads, and I have yet to get myself out of a fix by knowing the value of pi.

(True, I *did* say 'hypotenuse' once, but I meant something else.)

Public education should prepare us for life, not just tests; school should arm us with knowledge, not just information. Take, for instance, the timeless, burning question:

Why do guys act like that?

Our public education curriculum never prepares us for guys; specifically, American guys, who differ in many ways from guys in non-NASCAR countries. For example, in the culture of the graceful African Maasai, women all do the hard labor -- including, well, labor -- not to mention building their homes, cooking, cleaning, and driving off George Clooney.

So let's talk about guys. Take a moment to focus, and then have a go at our "What Would A Guy Do?" quiz.

And if your score's lousy, don't blame us. Blame public education.

~-~-~-~-~-~-~

Scenario: There are two grocers near your neighborhood. How does a guy choose between the two?
- A) High quality
- B) Low prices
- C) An aesthetically pleasing space designed to promote a leisurely inspection of fresh produce
- D) Distance from the parking lot to the beer

Scenario: What should a movie include to ensure that a guy will love it?

A) Cars
B) Women in cars
C) Women in cars, with weapons
D) Nearly-clothed, heavily armed, space alien gladiator women with massive, uh, glandular disorders

Scenario: What production element guarantees that a guy will hate a movie?

A) Subtitles
B) Subplots
C) Animated forest animals, unless they're heavily armed
D) Hugh Grant

Scenario: At the grocer's, there are forty-eight check-out lanes, of which three are actually open. All three are busy, to varying degrees. How does a guy calculate which lane he should use?

A) The one with the least customers
B) The one with the least overflowing carts
C) The one with the most magazines discussing drastic diets, ditzy Kardashians, and Hugh Grant
D) The one with the check-out clerk named Amber

Scenario: As advertisers have discovered, what does a guy consider to be a new car's most important selling point?

A) Great miles per gallon
B) Great safety ratings
C) Free pizza with any test drive
D) The car co-starred in a TV commercial, where it got hand-washed by a cheeseburger-eating blonde

Scenario: When shopping for a television, what technical feature is most important to a guy?

A) A crisp, bright picture
B) A long-lasting display
C) A remote control where, roughly, the number of buttons = pi
D) A screen the size of your average pre-industrial European nation

Scenario: To save a little time, a guy with just a few items in his basket decides to use the grocer's self-check-out. Of course, there's one item that won't scan correctly, because it was *never meant* to scan correctly, because the psychos who designed the whole self-check-out process are evil mutant space alien bridge trolls who hate Earth civilization and never trim their nose hair.

That was not part of the quiz - I just needed to get that off my chest.

Scenario: When it comes to job interviews, what is a guy's greatest fear?

A) An unattractive salary
B) An unattractive benefits package
C) An unattractive but flirty boss
D) An unattractive but flirty boss who's a guy

Scenario: When it comes to eating out alone, what is a guy's greatest fear?

A) The big-screen TVs might all be tuned to professional league bowling

B) Those pitying sidelong stares from other restaurant patrons

C) The dreaded self-Heimlich

D) That fight-or-flight moment at the salad bar when he contemplates just exactly why they call it a "sneeze guard"

Scenario: When it comes to eating out with a group of people, what is a guy's greatest fear?

A) Being asked to pronounce any entrée that has diacritical marks or words ending in 'eaux' or 'que'

B) Being asked to calculate the tip without consulting a computer

C) Being seated next to any guy involved in professional league bowling

D) Being seated next to any woman who subscribes to the pre-industrial European school of au naturel underarm self-expression

Scenario: According to the Creation story in the book of Genesis, God took a rib from Adam, the first guy. What happened to the rib?

A) It became Eve, Adam's helpmeet

B) It became Eve, whom Adam called the 'apple of my eye,' although *that* little term of endearment soured quickly

C) It became the first body part to be represented by celebrity divorce attorney Gloria Allred

D) No one really knows, but ever since then, guys have had this thing about barbecue

~-~-~-~-~-~

By the way: Initially, I didn't intend to just discuss guys. Initially, my topic was some of the major differences between males *and* females, but nobody I asked could agree on the female equivalent of the word *'guy.'*

To me, both *'girl'* and *'gal'* carry potential connotations that won't work. *'Ladies'* is corny, as is *'the other half.'* *'Distaff'* is pretentious; besides, half the people on Facebook would think I was talking about a stick. *'Sista'* would work, unless the discussion ever included my mother -- that sort of thing could send a guy spiraling into therapy.

One can't say *'babe,'* one can't say *'chick'* and, though it worked well once upon a time, one can no longer say *'dolls.'*

And don't *even* ask Rush Limbaugh what one can't say.

The Stupiding of America

(Would you, like, like fries with that?)

Everywhere you look lately, doomsayers and storm crows are keening about the end of the world. As evidence, they variously point to predictions, asteroids, scriptures, other storm crows, extremely pessimistic fortune cookies and, if you can believe it, a Central American rock.

And those are the "scientific" theories! Other jeremiads are more, well, let's say speculative. Kind of caroming between the miraculous and the maudlin. The internet is full of such theories, allegedly proving that the end is near:

- A Mayan calendar predicted the end of a 28,000 year rinse cycle
- Punxsutawney Phil saw his own shadow
- Punxsutawney Phil saw some *other* groundhog's shadow
- A Mayan calendar predicted the final season of *Meso-American Idol*

- In an Ozark grocery, someone claimed they saw Earth's picture on a milk carton
- Gas prices in Florida hit a spooky, all-time-high of $6.66
- Oprah gained forty pounds, and lost forty pounds, *in the same day*
- Bill O'Reilly's latest book was titled *Killing Lincoln, Kennedy, and Everybody Else*
- In a Memphis diner, someone spotted an omelet that looked like Elvis. Unfortunately, before it could be photo-documented, it was eaten by a guy that looked like Elvis.
- President Obama's ego saw its own shadow

But I have an alternative theory. I think we may simply be getting too stupid to survive. For example, look at some of the so-called "social" networks, like Facebook. Forget, for a moment, the content - it's so full of LOL, OMG, B4U, ROFLMAO, BTW, and RU2, it's hard to tell if you're having a conversation or collecting license plates.

Instead, take a notice, some time, of all the spelling suicides and grammatical train wrecks. Facebook now has an estimated 800 million users - that's more "residents" than most countries - and far too many FB'ers spell as if they're typing with their elbows.

And all the stupid isn't trapped online, either. It's in politics:
Here's an actual quote from a politician in a news interview: "I'm really gonna work really, really hard."
In case you missed the lead-in here - this was an adult, talking to an adult.

It's in the workplace:
Last year, I worked for a bipolar corporate dwarf for a brief period, though not nearly brief enough. Here's one of his little gems: "I just want to make sure everyone's singing Kumbaya on the same page."
Now that's stupid. Even for a dwarf.

It's in the shops:
Overheard by a youngster at a table at a fast food joint: "Omigod, like, ummm, these fries *so* taste like potatoes."
Yep. That's, like, America's future and stuff.

Nor are we waiting around to get bombarded by meteors, or rogue solar flares, or evil alien death rays. No, we're bombarding ourselves, daily, with some seriously sinister stuff. An endless barrage of mind-numbing messages, as deadly as anything conjured up by galactic bad guys.

No, not Adam Sandler movies. The *other* deadly stuff.

Commercials.

In commercials, life can be strange, confusing, even dangerous. But, here - I'll let *you* decide:

- You're expected to make critical purchasing decisions about bathroom tissue based on the endorsement of grinning, dancing, imaginary blue bears.
- If you attend anybody's wedding reception, you risk being cornered by a shortish woman who is obsessed with constipation. She also annoys passengers on planes.

- A company offering "do-it-yourself" pest control wants you to call them. Why?

- Happy young adults are running around in some farmer's field, making crop circles. And that's why you should buy potato chips in a tube.

- You're warned that a possible side-effect of your sleeping pill is "morning drowsiness." To the casual observer, this would seem to mean the sleeping pill didn't work.

- You should prefer a particular cell phone because it has "4G." 4G is a secret telecommunications enzyme that lets your cell phone morph into a lightning bolt you can throw like a spear.

- You're besieged daily with dire, cryptic threats about your intake of Bifidus Regularis, your supplemental levels of Ester-C, and your glycemic index. On the plus side, though, you must be getting wealthy, because now you have gout.

- You're encouraged to buy an anti-snoring device, although the thing looks like an oral appliance designed by Hannibal Lector. It may or may not keep *you* from snoring, but if you show up with that thing on your face, your partner definitely won't be.

- You watch helplessly as a man selling something he calls "liquid rubber in a can" cuts a hole in a rowboat, replaces the hole with a screen door, and then paddles around in the boat, grinning like someone who took a poison-tipped Mayan dart in the neck. What liquid rubber man *really* needs is some time in a rubber room.

- Someone wants you to buy a miracle device that will slice bread, handy for those among us who can't quite grasp that whole "sandwich" concept. These are probably the same people who need liquid soap in a dispenser, having not yet evolved to the point where they can be trusted with deceptively complex entities like bar soap.

- You need to buy gold, and you need to buy it right now, according to an extremely irritated G. Gordon Liddy, who has taken up the odd (but oddly reassuring) hobby of attacking stacks of American currency with a chain saw. I don't know about you, but when I need sound financial advice, I immediately riffle the Yellow Pages, looking for an indicted Watergate felon.

- Right now, there are people out there, perhaps people you live or work with, who are pondering calling a toll-free number so they can get a free hair analysis. Imagine the post-analysis debrief. "Yep. That's a hair, all right. Come on back next week - we're giving away a free eye exam!"

- Meanwhile, on TV, someone's son is being disciplined for riding his bike along his paper route and lobbing boxes of high-fiber cereal in neighbors' yards. OMG. Obviously, the truant has snapped, IMHO. Let's hope he doesn't own a rowboat and a screen door.

See what I mean? Kinda scary, huh? So let's get it together, America. It's time to de-stupid. Let's take control of our future...however much future we have left.

Because when 800 million people stop caring about intelligence, that can only lead to one thing.

More '*Die Hard*' sequels.

OMG.

Blowing Up & Other Fun Hobbies

(There's more than one definition of "traction")

There are a lot of things in America that I don't understand. Reality TV that isn't. Miracle cures that don't. Fast food that's neither. Soy milk. Wisconsin politics.

But right up there near the top of the list are weekend hobbies that cause you to catch on fire.

What I'm *not* talking about here is learning how to prepare blackened fish. I tried that once, too, in an apartment I was renting in Charleston. The apartment survived, and I didn't technically catch on fire, but I stood a good chance of getting arrested for murdering a security deposit.

What I *am* talking about is combustible-engine-based vehicle racing: that catch-all collection of off-road, on-road and near-road events, where people who like to drive too fast buy a bunch of beer, get together with a bunch of other people who like to drive too fast, buy more beer, and then proceed to thin out the

43

collective human herd by dying, and if the spectators are *really* lucky, exploding.

Maybe it's just me. I am probably what you would refer to as a "wimp," if you were a lumberjack, or a shark wrestler, or Sarah Palin. After all, my idea of a wild weekend is watching the uncensored "director's cut" of a 1930's Marx Brothers movie. (I know, I know - the societal implications of such unbridled hedonism are chilling. I would imagine your biggest fear in life is having an unmonitored maniac like me move into a house near your child's school.)

Now, I'm the first to admit that there's talent...not to mention bravery...involved in vehicle racing. After all, it takes keen reflexes and a dedicated focus just to survive a "civilian" morning commute...and that takes place on *public* roads. Just yesterday, in the shopping district of one of South Carolina's metro areas, police identified the atrophied body of a driver who had been unsuccessfully attempting to make a left turn across incoming traffic since 1968.

But, speaking in a classical sense, there's bravery involved in putting your hand on a hot stove. Sadly, though, after you're done, there's nothing much left but discipline, as you learn to spell your name with your other hand.

So I can admire the challenge; I just don't get the cheering. I appreciate the skill, but not the thrill. I fail to appreciate the attraction of driving around in circles, much less watching *other* people drive around in circles.

If wanted to pointlessly rush around in circles, I'd go to work.

And why so many circuits around the same oval? I mean, it's not like the race officials are moving the tarmac around, pushing up moguls and gouging pot-holes in-between laps. Come to think of it, that would make things much more interesting. After all, even in professional golf, they occasionally move the holes around. And golf has been mathematically proven to be the most boring spectator sport in the known Universe, except for bowling, or watching Geraldo Rivera inject himself into breaking news.

It's true, of course, that thoroughbreds and greyhounds are often forced to run around in circles, as if they were filing health insurance claims, but at least the horses and hounds get to stop after completing the lap. (The greyhounds, however, have been justifiably irritated ever since some do-gooder leaked the news that, all this time, they've been chasing a fake rabbit on a stick.)

Now, I understand that there are millions of vehicle racing fans, spanning all social and cultural segments, and they may have insider insights to which I am not privy. I also understand that, since we're talking about loud, outdoor public events that involve beer, I could spend the next half-hour coming up with "privy" jokes. And, of course, many professional vehicle racing events involve the participation of nearly-clad women, who apparently can earn a decent living by wearing a bikini, stiletto heels and a sash that promotes motor oil, while tip-toeing around on a bunting-laced platform and waving giant bowling trophies.

I guess I'm just overly cautious. Personally, I wouldn't make it through day one at Vehicle Racing School.

_-~-~-~-~-_

INSTRUCTOR: Hello, class, and welcome to Day One of our summer elective, *How To Drive In A Counter-Clockwise Circle Without Dying Much*! My name's Parnell. Please sign these legal disclaimers.

MODERATELY OBSERVANT STUDENT: Where's your other leg?

INSTRUCTOR: Today, we're going to discuss Voluntary Immolation! First, we'll watch a short training film entitled, "Learning To Write With Your Good Hand," and then we'll head outside to the track, measure you for your flame-resistant Abrasion Minimizing suit, and strap you in to the cage.

(Sound of Barry's receding footfalls)

_-~-~-~-~-_

As part of my exhaustive research for this column, I spent almost five whole minutes on the internet, where I discovered many websites that cater to these weekend warriors, or to their eventual medical needs. In order to hammer home their sales pitch, most of these websites are heavily dependent upon very bold graphics, very bold air-brushed photos of nearly-clad women, and staggeringly obvious typos. For some reason, I never expected in this life to be able to include ... in the same shopping cart ... a set of tires, an in-dash CD changer, a collision restraint system, a 10-vial "party pak" of nitrous oxide, and a self-activating fire extinguisher.

See, to me, that's a great huge clue. Never select a hobby that involves *both* compressed explosive gases *AND* volunteer fire department supplies. This is what seasoned pundits would call a

46

"self-fulfilling prophesy" or, roughly translated into street-speak, what the rest of us would call "rock stupid."

In my own defense, may I point out that I come by my caution honestly. Several years ago, during a nice lake weekend with friends, I learned by accident how to not parasail. I've shared that story with you before, and I won't bore you with it here. Let's just say that, if you ever decide to try parasailing for the first time, don't try it with a boat pilot who's also trying boat-piloting for the first time.

And you may want to invest in a custom-fitted Abrasion Minimizer.

Full Frontal Stupidity

Bread and Circuses

(We'll be right back to our commercials after this brief game!)

Picture it: Thundering noise erupts and bubbles in the Coliseum. Thudding, unseen drums pound out a hypnotic heartbeat as rank after rank of bronze-girded warrior slaves slog into the arena, bearing a mighty flaxen-haired Queen, masked by a screen of giant feathers fetched from some monstrous mythical raptor. The eager, madding congregation pulses with anticipation, hungering for the long-awaited Queen. Suddenly, she rises above her captive coterie and unleashes her...

...polyester pompoms.

And that was just the Patriots' backup quarterback.

Super Bowl XLVI. In case you missed it, it was actually a pretty good commercial, if you could stand all the game interruptions. And with an obscene price tag like seven million dollars per commercial minute, I'm surprised they bothered to show the actual game at all.

According to this year's Super Bowl pre-game show, which began approximately XII minutes after last year's Super Bowl, Madonna was slated to perform, but only at halftime. Fans could hardly wait to see the superstar singer at Super Bowl XLVI, even though she's now VII years older than the Super Bowl itself. However, she's still Madonna and guys are still guys. So, before the game, to keep the athletes and fans focused on the game, she agreed to be dipped in saltpeter.

As for the commercials, all the usual suspects were there - the beer Clydesdales, the cola Polar Bears in red scarves, Elton John in his street clothes.

But the Super Bowl commercials have gotten so complex, so over-produced, so...well, so Hollywood, we don't know what they're selling. They're not very clever ads anymore - they're just very short movies. They're just high-budget, star-studded, non-feature-length films. Now I'm watching a movie, not making a shopping list.

Other than the occasional familiar face (see "Clydesdales"), I can no longer remember what product(s) they're pushing. And even *then*, I don't know. I don't know if the horses are hauling Bud, or Bud Lite, or Bud Light Platinum, Bud Super-Extra-Light, Bud Flashlight, Bud Light Saber, Bud Extra Premium Ultralite Acolyte, Bud Disguised As Michelob, or Buddy Ebsen. Are those mute, nearly-naked, ice-skating polar bears strung out on Coke? Or New Coke? Original Coke? Coke Zero? Coke Too Low For Zero? Bud Disguised As Coke? Meth? (see "ice-skating naked")

Here, I'll let *you* decide. Here are a few actual Super Bowl commercials -- the plot and then the pitch. *You* tell *me* who's selling what:

The Plot: Polar bears that wear scarves and watch television sometimes have to walk away and yell in the night to relieve their angst.
The Pitch: Drink our cola!
~-~-~-~-~-~-~

The Plot: Due a some unnamed disaster that apparently involved Ford trucks, everyone in the world is dead, except for nine nondescript rednecks.
The Pitch: Buy a Chevy!
~-~-~-~-~-~-~

The Plot: Sometimes our employees run around in a warehouse and throw paint balloons at a wall, perpetually grinning as if they had some kind of mandible disorder.
The Pitch: Fly our airline!
~-~-~-~-~-~-~

The Plot: A grandmother launches a small child from a slingshot, in order to steal food from an obnoxious brat in a tree house.
The Pitch: Eat our corn chips!
~-~-~-~-~-~-~

Then we watched a commercial starring naked M&Ms in a disco.

Naked candy.

We should've known. We should've seen it coming. If pole-dancing chocolate managed to make it past the censors, halftime was gonna be a full-on Caligula moment.

~-~-~-~-~-~

And then, Halftime. Sic infit. We should've known.

After Madonna flashed her polyester pompoms from atop her bare beer bier (see "Bud Light"), she walked across a bridge of bronzed centurion-ish extras to the stage, where she proceeded to not really sing and not really dance, while only tripping once. (Which still impressed *me*. Madonna and I are the same age and I tripped more than that just walking to the fridge for more queso. And nobody paid *me* to sing; in fact, like Madonna, I'm often paid *not* to.)

Overall, the halftime show was a non-threatening event. We did have to put up with some infantile Brit twit named AWOL, who showed her appreciation for being invited to perform at the world's most-watched TV show by flipping off 111 million viewers. If that's her attitude, she might as well move here and run for Congress.

And all the costume changes confused me. Romans, Brits, Pharaohs, choirs. I wasn't sure if Madonna was invading the Vatican, annexing Egypt, or channeling Hannibal.

In one particularly obscure segue, this Richard Simmons-type character began crotch-bouncing on some kind of semi-tightrope thing (I've since learned that it's called a Slack Wire). Every time I think about it, I still wince and want to assume the fetal position. Had that been me on the Slack Wire, the bidding for my remains would've been a battle between the Vienna Boys Choir and Tyson's Deluxe Chicken Parts (Lite). Sans nuggets.

For the record, the looming threat of a "Wardrobe Malfunction" never materialized. This was fortunate, particularly for NBC's defense attorneys, though it was unfortunate for fifteen-year-olds, or those in charge of America's foreign policy with Iran, which is the same thing, except fifteen-year-olds have more common sense.

We all recall that infamous event during Super Bowl XLVI minus VIII, when Janet Jackson only displayed a breast for IX-XVIths of a second, forcing men everywhere to rush out and buy a TiVo so they could auto-loop.

It was the ultimate instant replay, not to mention history's most monitored mammogram.

Not to worry. This year, we didn't have to collectively blush when someone's yay slipped out of her boostie. This year, we were treated to a much more elegant act.

Right.

This year, we just stared at SNAFU's one-finger salute, waited for somebody somewhere to sing a decipherable syllable or two, and watched a stageful of prone, nearly-clad women repeatedly thrusting their navels in the air, as if they'd just laid back on a rogue heating pad or an overcooked Hot Pocket.

But all unholy spectacles must come to an end...especially when seven million blings are at stake.

~-~-~-~-~-~-~

The Plot: A mutant two-headed black man argues with his other head, which then sings in falsetto.
The Pitch: Buy our dependable German car!

~-~-~-~-~-~-~

The Plot: Youngish vampires are at a campfire party in the woods, waiting for an undead pusher to show up with some blood. Dead Dude arrives and pulls a bag of plasma out of the glove box. Suddenly, all the vampires explode.
The Pitch: Buy our luxury Japanese car!

~-~-~-~-~-~-~

The Plot: An incontinent kid relieves himself in a swimming pool.
The Pitch: Use our tax software!

~-~-~-~-~-~-~

The Plot: A sultry foreigner dresses herself in public, then mumbles something unintelligible in an accent so thick it could stop ants.
The Pitch: Order our flowers!

~-~-~-~-~-~-~

The Plot: Jaded young people standing in line on a city street suddenly erupt into song and dance and are joined by emaciated rock guitarists, chunky gospel choirs, and stuntmen, as if the

Occupy Wall Street scab warriors had mated with the cast of Glee during an audition for a movie by Quentin Tarantino.
The Pitch: Switch to our phone plan!
~-~-~-~-~-~-~

Did Arby's, those "roast beef" guys, really just spend 3.5 million bucks to promote a fried fish sandwich?
~-~-~-~-~-~-~

And so it ended. Football season is now officially over. Now, sports fans eagerly move on to that action-packed, Olympian crowd-pleaser...

Bowling.

Moriituri semi Brunswickia liga te salutant. (*We who are about to face a VII-X split salute you.*)
~-~-~-~-~-~-~

By the way - before this year's game, one sponsor proudly announced that "aerial coverage of tonight's Super Bowl" would be brought to you by Bud Light.

Aerial coverage.

Of a game that was being played in an enclosed building. With a roof. That doesn't retract.

Thanks a lot, Bud.

White-Collar Infractions (The Workplace)

~*~*~

"Committee -- a group of the unwilling, picked from the unfit, to do the unnecessary."

Richard Harkness

~*~*~*~*~

Full Frontal Stupidity

Scenes From a Maul

(Full-contact shopping, American style)

Last weekend, I went to a hockey game, and a Black Friday sale broke out.

Ah. We must be getting on toward Christmas. That magical time of year when we wrap and exchange gifts, visit with family and friends, and blast defenseless toy store shoppers in the face with pepper spray.

What in the world is going on with these discount-stalking holiday shoppers? These Black Friday blackguards? I've seen better-behaved people at a Hannibal Lector reunion.

Now, to be sure, we ought to have seen it coming. After all, retailers have been building a Frankenstein monster for years. Impatiently pacing behind the curtain, during all that warm Thanksgiving festivity, there's been this contrived, frenzied, marketing-induced mania associated with the day *after* Thanksgiving. Slowly, inexorably, retailers have reinforced the idea that if you're not out there shopping on Black Friday, then you are an ice troll who makes children drink schnapps and doesn't love house pets.

Shame on you! Good people - decent, patriotic people - they get out there on Black Friday in support of truth, justice and Early Bird discounts.

And this year, the Greed That Stole Christmas couldn't even wait till Friday morning to lay lures. They couldn't wait till Black Friday to do Black Friday. Stores started teasing, daring us to *not* show up by 6am ... then 4am ... 1am ... midnight ... ultimately, they had Friday on Thursday. And only because Wednesday was already gone.

Hang on. At this rate, next year we'll have Black June.

If we can wait till June.

By the way - the pepper spray attack? That actually happened, at a mega-box store on the West Coast. Some dedicated shoppinista, working on reliable intelligence from her forward reconnaissance patrol, identified and vectored a high-value target - a shrink-wrapped pallet of undefended Nintendo Wii. (or Wee, or Whee, or Huiee, or however you correctly misspell it)

Sergeant Majorette accepted her mission. She knew the score, she knew the cost. Collateral damage was acceptable. She bivouacked and waited, repeatedly mumbling her mission:

Purchase, with extreme prejudice.

The rest was reflex. When the indigenous military began to unwra ... uh, sorry ... when the store's staff began to unwrap the goods, the alleged lunatic allegedly whirled around, whipped out her handy Girl-on-the-Go-sized pepper spray, and wasted the other Wii hopefuls. Then she pocketed the purchase and escaped into a rabid crowd that was busily disemboweling a late-arriving FedEx panel truck. Later, she annexed Poland.

In another ugly incident, a shopper was arrested for attacking an innocent clerk at a "Returns" counter. Apparently, the dissatisfied patron had just purchased a new smartphone app, the iSleep 3000, which provides a library of sounds guaranteed to help battle insomnia (you know, taped loops of rain, waves, chirping birds, street traffic, Al Gore speeches). According to the poor clerk, the patron went into a blind rage after discovering that the "Sound of Cicadas" option was only available every seventeen years.

Of course, I wasn't there. I heard about all this random consumer violence from the newspaper, the Hair Helmets anchoring the TV news, and a few eye-witness accounts from recovering survivors. I personally didn't shop on Black Friday because, well, because I'm scared. And there is no product on the market, made by any company on the planet, for which I am willing to lose actual body parts.

I'm not unreasonably spineless, mind you. When I go shopping, I'm prepared to face a bit of inconvenience, and I'm prepared to face down an acceptable level of violence. For example, I'm as prepared as any other grown man to get chewing gum stuck to my shoe. I am *not* ready to get mace-blinded by some 300-pound, eight-jelly-sandwich-eating, high-torque Aunt wearing purple-and-peach-striped spandex and sequined flip-flops, all over a $2 DVD copy of *Star Wars - The Musical.*

And I'm not even talking about your garden variety "check-out line" violence, where one naturally expects a few bruises, some insults, and sixty-eight magazines featuring Kardashian-type mammals caught in various stages of odd behavior (and even odder poses). I'm talking about violence out in the product aisles.

Basically, I like to keep violence at arm's distance, and I wouldn't mind having longer arms. I prefer to limit my mayhem exposure to manageable arenas, like "New Release" day at a video store near a trailer park, or visiting the all-you-can-shovel-down Chinese buffet just after Sunday church in a Southern town. But I'll pass on that intense, armed, Black Friday level of focused, gauntlet-running chaos.

I suppose it's worth pointing out that the vast majority of these "Customer Slays Nine" headlines were generated inside great, huge box stores with names like Sprawl-Mart, Worst Imaginable Buy, and Pan-Asian Slave Labor Sweatshop Outlet-R-Us. That may be pure coincidence. I have no empirical evidence that points to a causal relationship between crazed zombie-like violence and Montana-sized enclosures full of substandard, imported lead-laced teething rings. I'm just saying.

And, as with any psychotic episode worth its prescription hallucinogenics, there were participants who didn't fit the mold. In a TV ad, I saw a nice, tranquil lady shopping in some department store. She calmly approached her desired item, lifted it from the shelf, placed it in her shopping cart, and calmly moved on. Why wasn't she running madly to the next item on her list? Why was she not hobbling nearby shoppers with a modified price labeling gun?

Shameful, it is. Obviously, this woman doesn't love her family very much.

Full Frontal Stupidity

Pets Are People, Too

(Hey! Who you callin' a dumb animal?)

I used to work for an acceptably neurotic American company. But then they bought a dwarf, so I had to move on.

It wasn't the dwarf's fault, of course. Imaginary characters with pointy hats have to eat, too. But I had to get out while I could; while I was still rational. I mean, a dwarf can be handy, no doubt about it, particularly on days when you've taken all you can stand and you just need to throw something.

But there are limits to the capabilities of a dwarf, even a corporate dwarf. A dwarf is not management material - it just smells like it. And if, for whatever cloudy, muddled middle-management reason, you give a dwarf its own office, it's only a matter of time before co-workers start listening to it; before it starts scheduling meetings; before it begins calling you in for weekly "one-on-one's." And before you know it, people start to believe that the dwarf is capable of normal human behaviors - complex cerebral machinations, like hiding your wallet in the toe of your shoe at the beach, or saying "thank you" after getting a speeding ticket. Complex behaviors that indicate higher intelligence.

After all, we're talking about a dwarf.

The term, I think, is anthropomorphism. But that's big word to be lifting without having warmed up first. Be warned not to toss it about carelessly; think twice before shoving it in the middle of a heated argument. You don't just wade into a word like anthropomorphism - you could lose a tooth.

For some background, *anthropomorphism* is listed in the dictionary as a noun. And I understand that, if you're the type of person who has Facebook as your home page, the previous sentence may contain several confusing words, including "dictionary" and "noun." ("Background," I'll give you. Benefit of the doubt.)

According to my copy of "The 2011 Public Sector Union-Approved Book Of, Like, Words And Stuff," *anthropomorphism* is the attribution of human qualities to non-human things, like pets, or machines, or politicians. In other words, it's the act of treating a dog (or a dwarf) like a person; of expecting raptors to have a conscience, or expecting members of Congress to have a digestive system.

You've seen anthropomorphism in action, hundreds of times. People will wave at a goldfish, or gob baby-talk at a cat, or put a knit hat on a Doberman. Housewives will coax a stubborn dishwasher, commuters will curse a spent car battery, clueless office clerks will try and bribe a misbehaving spreadsheet, frustrated sales reps will kick a dwarf.

But where it really gets out of control is when people subject their pets to blisteringly inhumane, criminally insulting acts of random cuteness. We've already mentioned a particularly foul example - knit hats on dogs.

It gets worse.

Now hang on to something. Know, gentle reader, that you can buy little booties for your dog to wear when you all go camping. And if you can buy them, that means there's a market for them.

It gets worse.

You can also buy a little matching "Canine Camper" backpack, ergonomically adjusted for Fifi or Fido.

That's just sad.

Picture the scene. As the poor pup's owners (Chaz and Trixine) are busily trying to extract the backpack from its sadistic molded-plastic sarcophagus, Bowser must be anthropomorphically rolling his eyes and thinking, "Oh, I'm not believin' this. Matching backpack? What's up with *that*? I'm still nauseous over the *hat*. Look, bipeds, I wouldn't be caught dead in this *AT HOME*. But we get out in the wilderness and you suddenly go all Stupid Pet Tricks on me?"

For all I know, there's a matching fold-out butane stove and arf-activated color-coordinated canteen. (monogram not included)

It gets worse.

In some coastal communities ... I forget which ... public safety officials are using dogs as shark-spotters. Again, I forget which coast, but I'm guessing it's California. In Florida, all dogs are either auditioning in Orlando to understudy Pluto or Scooby Doo, or else they're frantically trying to avoid Vietnamese restaurants.

North of the Florida line, most dogs are gainfully employed as pets, or assisting Homeland Security in not enforcing immigration laws, or modeling Sierra Club knit hats. (In-between jobs, they can be found killing a little time randomly fertilizing my yard. Apparently, they have a map.)

But on the coast, callous humans are using clueless canines to spot sharks. Since the dogs don't realize what they've been asked to do, and since they probably never saw "Jaws," I assume it works like this: the dogs hop around in the mid-height surf until they spot something swimming by that looks suspiciously like a long grey cat, or a very plump dwarf. A genetic response fires in the dog, and it leaps around, thrashing and making food-like noises, until the shark has its *own* genetic response, which involves lots of aquatic dental work, and which I won't discuss here in front of children, or Facebook users. Let's just say that, last week, when Sparky the shark-spotter's owners went shopping for four "Backwoods Booties" and a canteen, I hope they kept the sales receipt.

What is it, exactly, that we expected the dog to do? Eyeball the antediluvian predator, maybe, make a quick calculation, then turn to the lifeguard and mutter, "You're gonna need a bigger boat."

It gets worse.

Ponder, human, *this* horrifying thought. You realize, don't you, that somewhere ... right now ... somewhere out there are the five humiliated dogs who were forced to pose for the original "dogs playing poker" velvet painting? What were we thinking? What shame! How do these poor dogs look themselves in the mirror, assuming they know what a mirror is, and how to look in one, if they had access to one, or borrowed a friend's, maybe to adjust their knit hat, or to discuss reflective optics?

And now, everywhere there's an empty lot on a busy street, some human is profiting from the sale of these paintings, along with their poor cousin, "dogs playing pool," and the obligatory assortment of oversized velvet paintings that always seem to feature Elvis, an attractive dark-skinned couple with huge Afros, or a dwarf dressed up like a matador.

Shameful. As the "top of the food chain" around these parts, we really ought to ease up on the animal kingdom. Think before you act. Pets are people, too.

Just this week, I read a Facebook posting from someone named Amber. Based on her "profile," I thought Amber was a cute, perky legal assistant with some kind of out-of-control lung edema. As it turns out, "Amber" is an ex-con who lives up a spur road outside of Tucson, collects commemorative railroad plates, and cross-breeds pit bulls for resale to California lifeguards. But that's not the point.

Amber was all excited because he or she was preparing for their annual pig roast. Every year, it seems, Amber and his or her family invite people over, and they cook a pig. Every year.

Don't you know that must get old for the pig.

Think, people. We can't just keep kicking these animals around.

After all, we're not talking about a dwarf.

The Many Advantages of Not Working From Home

(For every cloud lining, there's some silver nitrate)

Today, I killed a man. But that's okay.

It was an unfortunate (but necessary) social adjustment, but it's going to be fine, because it took place in the "abandon all hope" left-turn lane of a confused intersection on a criminally-overcrowded six-lane strip of commercial pavement, chock-full of insane commuters, during the daily American gonzo gauntlet known as the "morning rush hour."

So it could be six or eight weeks before anybody slows down long enough to notice the body.

Some of you readers already know about my recent shift back into the work-a-day world, the on-site, five-days-a-week, corporate-American labor pool, and my on-going struggle to adapt. So for you, this is not breaking news. On the other hand, very little that I write, ever, qualifies as actual news. For one thing, I don't have nearly enough money in my Hair Helmet budget to honestly be considered as a viable, professional news biped.

And if you're a paid subscriber to my weekly "opinion" columns, let me first say this: you're lying. I don't *have* any paid subscribers. If you really are paying somebody for the "privilege" of reading my weekly columns, you're paying somebody else. That's fine with me, and ultimately, if someone has figured out how to con both you *and* me, I'm happy for the evil little criminal rat scum jerk. I just thought you should know that you're the patsy in a scam of colossal proportions, like ethanol, or automatic payroll deductions.

But one must eat, and one must wear clothes, unless one is a member of Congress. So, in order to remain clothed and fed, one must do what one must do ... one must follow the rules, one must do the right thing, unless one is a member of Congress. That means that we must learn to adjust to new things, to find the good in bad things, to seek the divine in all things, and to keep going to work so we can keep buying more things.

To be sure, working from home parades its allures. Yes, it's fun and safe, it's comfortable, it's familiar and productive, it's convenient and includes easy access to music and beer, and it demands absolutely no expense whatsoever from the employer. But we're already into Paragraph Seven, so let's not drag logic into this.

And it's in that non-bitter, mature adult spirit that I offer you the following list. Like me, you may find yourself faced with the need to actually get in your car and drive to work. But you might not yet have fully pondered some of your blessings. Partly, that's because these blessings are hidden, though mostly, it's because I'm lying. But let's not niggle.

So what are some of these hidden blessings?

Witness:

- When you work from home, you sacrifice many opportunities to hone your guerilla warfare tactics. Among its other benefits, the unexpected inter-departmental interactions that are rife in an office environment can keen your senses and reflexes in a way that no home office can match. For example, when working from home and deep in concentration on some puzzling software problem, I almost *never* have someone leap out of the tree-line behind me, bound up to my chair and bark, "SCUSE ME. YOU BUSY?"

- Any office environment worth its salt will eventually devolve into a brisk, brutal game of Thermostat Wars. I think there must be a law - every multi-human workspace must contain at least one person, caught up in some kind of post-menopausal flop sweats, who is constantly carping about the heat, and another person who is forever freezing to death. As such, the rest of the room's occupants spend their days watching the Fahrenheit Foes attempt to surreptitiously sneak the common area's thermostat up, or down, a few degrees. To be fair to the caloric combatants, their discomfort is partly due to the dynamics of the room itself, which for some reason was designed to support a full-blown pizza oven on one side of the room and Walt Disney's cryogenic vault on the other.

- Now, let's move on to time-wasting tactics. If you work from home, you're on your own. It's now entirely up to you to figure out how to completely blow a perfectly good hour every morning, and another hour every afternoon. Were you commuting to work every day like everybody else, these two dead-and-gone chunks of your life could have been wasted far more unproductively, sitting through multiple traffic-light cycles in an expensive, pollution-spewing, multi-ton, fiscally-depreciating device, where you would learn from fellow commuters how to employ a modified version of American Sign Language that efficiently culls the communication toolbox down to a single finger. And the spatial measurement skills you'd learn, navigating rush hour lane changes, would go far in preparing you for any post-Armageddon, Mad Max-ish dead-Earth environments, should someone like Qaddafi finally run out of silly hats, get bored, and start randomly punching Korean-labeled buttons on his compound's office console.

- And though we've already discussed the work commute, it's so spectacularly foul tha ... um ... I mean, it's so spectacularly productive that it can stand another, um, uh, treatment. Not only does the drive to work (and from work) present a great prospect for hating (or being hated); the savvy commuter will spot college-course-level opportunities to observe the human beast in its unnatural environment. Next time you're out on the turnpike tundra, keep an eye out for not-so-rare sightings of Freeway Fauna: the musical antics of the Faux Rock-Idol Dashboard Smacker; the drone-like determination of the Myopic Speed Limit Pedant, the frantic feeding habits of the Drive-Thru Dropped-Crumb Pie-Hole Vulture, the Rearview-Preening Mama Grizzly; the Paw-Gesturing Carpool Chatter-Beast; the dreaded iPhone-y Larynx-Warbler.

- For technical and legal reasons, I spend very little time in the Ladies' Room. So I'm not qualified to proffer commentary on that most inner of sancta. But, as a general rule, the male version of the public bathroom has to be seen to be believed, and preferably from an upwind vector. It's a public space that looks a lot like some of the less-well-funded parts of Eastern Europe might have looked, on the afternoon after the Black Plague. Management's decorative motif and maintenance plan seem to have run along the lines of "Bathroom? We own a bathroom?" Somewhere near the sink, there will be damaged dispenser dripping some viscous something in an odd shade of sci-fi green (tellingly labeled Ye Old Soappe) and by the door there will be a trashcan that was last emptied to honor our national heroes at the Alamo. There's usually at least one semi-detached "seating appliance" that seems to have been drop-kicked by some violent commuter who just lost his pet ferret to the Black Plague. In your average public men's room, you'll find anaerobic cultures that have not yet been catalogued by the World Health Organization. Granted, they're microscopic cultures, but they're not nearly microscopic enough.

- And finally, there's the bizarre (but highly anticipated) weekly custom we call "Casual Friday." As far as I can tell, this is some kind of low-maintenance semi-mating ritual in which employees are encouraged to act out their full pantheon of personal American liberties by "dressing down." It seems a participatory, collective effort to dance right up to the edge of codified indecent exposure, without actually crossing over the line into legally actionable lewd public display, or Roman Polanski auditions. Of course, I could be wrong (I gave up semi-mating long ago). Maybe it's just a simple submission to a brutal reality. After all, the ultimate weekly horror is upon the workforce - the Friday afternoon rush hour is looming, and nobody wants to bleed on their good shirt.

So hang in there, America, play the game, and learn to have some fun with it.

After all ... as the Rolling Stones have advised, "You can't always get what you want. But if you try, sometimes, you just might find you get what you need, minus automatic payroll deductions."

The Turbeaux Diaries

(Reflections on corporate taxonomy, if not outright taxidermy)

I call him Turbeaux. That's not his real name, of course. A dwarf generally has a first and last name, just like you and me, unless the dwarf is dumb enough to lose one of his names (it happens more often than you might think). And Turbeaux was an exceptionally stupid dwarf.

Even for a corporate dwarf.

As we know from several songs, sung by people who are now dead, "life goes on." And mine has. But before the memory fades - or before my psyche blocks out the whole episode as part of a protective auto-defense mechanism - let me tell you about my summer with the dwarf.

It's a fairly standard tale, I suppose, to those of you who have figured out how to go to work every day, week after week, surrounded by walls and waste and weird report requests and unwarranted office rearrangements and mandatory pencil requisitions in triplicate and Secret Santas and corporate dwarves - and then do it again, and again, all without going clinically insane.

So I'll attempt to not bore you with my bit of a tale, partly by interspersing a few flashbacks from my diary, which I maintained during my days in the company of a company's bi-polar dwarf.

Witness...

DEAR DIARY: Today, at work, the dwarf got disoriented during our weekly "Chip & Dale Carnegie" motivational meeting. As a result of his confusion, the dwarf rescheduled his secretary's schedule so she could work the "paradigm shift."

See? That's the kind of nonsense I had to deal with, earlier this year, when I found myself working with ... and then working for ... a bi-polar dwarf. Or course, we didn't call him Turbeaux at first. That came later.

DEAR DIARY: Today, the dwarf was late for work. Turns out he'd let his shampoo confuse him and then he got caught in a vicious "lather, rinse, repeat" loop.

DEAR DIARY: Today, at lunch, somebody convinced the dwarf that he couldn't possibly get salmonella, because he wasn't eating salmon. So now we know: a bi-polar dwarf with food poisoning turns a really weird shade of green.

As you might imagine, being barely taller than a grade-school ruler presents its own problems for a dwarf, especially when you're a corporate dwarf swaggering around and burdened with that deadliest of combinations: a middle-management job title and a very short fuse.

DEAR DIARY: Today, at work, the dwarf went ballistic after learning that normal-height people use these things called "light switches," and that's what actually makes the lights go on and off. Until now, the dwarf had thought meeting rooms were just sad to see him leave.

DEAR DIARY: Today, at work, a tall woman accused the dwarf of staring at her knees. The dwarf, of course, pouted and whined, saying he preferred women half her thighs.

Turbeaux had learned to simultaneously suck up *and* pout, which of course qualified him for a middle-management position, his own office, and keys to the corporate lunchroom. The dwarf didn't eat much, though; he somehow acquired nourishment from attending endless meetings and parroting drivel like "you're so right, Bill" and "paradigm shift."

Turbeaux is mad for meetings. (That's how he got the nickname "Turbeaux." Think "Tasmanian Devil" armed with a quiver of Venn Diagrams.) Turbeaux will schedule an afternoon meeting to talk about planning a meeting to analyze that morning's meeting, that he had convened to discuss the inordinate amount of non-productive time middle-management's been spending in meetings.

DEAR DIARY: Today, at work, while loping from one meeting to the next, the dwarf ran into another wall. For the rest of the day, he walked around cupping a seashell to his head. When asked why, he said he'd been advised to file an injury claim, and somebody told him if you hold a seashell next to your ear, you could hear OSHA (he really is a very stupid dwarf).

DEAR DIARY: Today, at work, the dwarf had another "green" epiphany, and confiscated everybody's Earth-killing light bulbs. Sadly, though, his little corporate dwarf cranium had forgotten to buy replacement bulbs, so he had to redistribute our originals. Of course, the rest of us worked *that* little "gift" all day long. We spent the rest of the day complaining that we had to work using somebody else's light.

Right about now, you may find yourself thinking about some of the middle-management characters at *your* office. Hmmm. Could Fred in Purchasing be a bi-polar dwarf? Hmmm. Sure, that Angela in Accounts Payable is taller than a fire hydrant, but ... might a dwarf run out and purchase shoe inserts? Hmmm?

DEAR DIARY: Today, at work, a rogue "who's your secret gift partner" email exploded, destroying half of the dwarf's moustache. At least, I hope that's what happened to his moustache. I'd hate to think the little guy walks around looking like that on purpose.

DEAR DIARY: Today, at work, the dwarf inexplicably insisted that everybody start referring to him as "The Hammer," possibly because he's exactly the same height as one. Unimpressed co-workers just let him rave on, and on and on, until he finally fainted from a hubris overload. Then we all rolled him into a corner and voted on whether to keep calling him "Turbeaux," or to just stick with our current pet name, "Irrelevant Yard Ornament."

Of course, a middle-management corporate dwarf with a job title is still a member of middle-management, with all the petty, vindictive, destructive, career-warping power that such a position confers.

And as I was about to learn, you can only push a bi-polar dwarf so far.

DEAR DIARY: Today, at work, I switched some characters on the dwarf's keyboard. As a result, a huge client got an email, inviting them to fake their sales witch at a Friday seminal.

That was the beginning of the end.

And then, one day, the dwarf got terminally angry at me because, according to him, I didn't look at him often enough when he was "making a point." (a.k.a. shrieking, throwing extremely light objects at people's knees, and pulse-popping the few remaining veins in his Malibu Barbie-sized forehead)

Yeah, I know. I thought the same thing you're thinking right now. A corporate dwarf, in a position of tiny-step-ladder-assisted authority, mad at me because I didn't look at him enough.

Whoa.

You know, as part of my initial conversations with this company, Mrs. H.R. Lady had submitted me to a psychiatric evaluation.

Standard stuff, nothing invasive, no dials or restraints, no goofy paper outfits that never quite close in the back, thereby allowing you to simultaneously freeze to death while letting you advertise your spine and, um, points south.

A standard psych analysis. Just a last-chance, optimistic opportunity for the Human Resources department to weed out the finger chewers, the criminally insane, and other members of Congress.

I got the job, so obviously, I evaluated as "sane." Obviously, Turbeaux also slipped one past the goalie.

And obviously, the Psychiatric Evaluation Metrics review committee of the Federated Union of Human Resources needs to reassess their standards.

But life goes on, and now I'm unemployed again.

Have I learned anything, you ask? Well, yeah. Sure, I've learned something. Two things, actually:

1. From what I know of psych exams, most of corporate America could very well be insane.
2. If you ever need to take out a dwarf, you can't necessarily depend on salmonella.

Turn Left...um...Eventually

(The continuing race toward an adjective-free America)

I don't have a normal hobby, like collecting stamps, or training pit bulls to chew each other and write their name so they can sign their royalty checks over to NFL quarterbacks. But I do like to keep the old mental faculties well-oiled. So this week, I learned several new ways to get sued.

Now, don't scoff. Some of the ways I learned to get sued are pretty bizarre (literal translation: "the government must be involved"). For example, I can now get sued for phone malpractice!

What did *you* do this week? Can *you* get sued for phone malpractice?

What I'm talking about, of course, is that even-more-than-normally-simple-minded government program known as the Fair Housing Act.

Now, before you pop a blood vessel and start suing me for just *talking* about suing me, let me point out that I have nothing against the construction or intent of the original Fair Housing Act in 1968, nor its 1988 upgrade (Fair Housing, Version 2.0, civil Service Pack 3).

But what began as an honorable attempt to insure equality has, of course, mutated. It has morphed beyond recognition - as unchecked, overfunded government programs inevitably do - into that dread ghoul, that beast which cannot be fed.

Political Correctness.

Case in point. Let's say you're someone who owns an apartment complex. As you might imagine, potential tenants will call you. Hopefully. Otherwise, you will soon be someone who once owned an apartment complex.

That's not entirely true, of course. Rather than failing at owning an apartment complex, and then gracefully going out of business to try something else, you could just change your name from "Casa Del Mescalito Horizon Forest Manor Acres" to "Casa Del Mescalito Horizon Forest Manor Acres Savings & Loan," run out and buy a big money rake, and wait for the harvest. Or you could masquerade as a California solar panel manufacturer, collect Star Wars battle-cruiser-sized loads of taxpayer cash, and then go out of business. (Oddly enough, these criminals *never* get sued).

But for now, while you're still running the apartment complex, potential tenants will call you. They'll call you for floor plan descriptions, square footage measurements, Management's views on concealed weapons permits, prices, deposits, directions, and to inquire about permission to bring their "baby," Lurker, a 285-pound Argentine Dogo with the larynx of a ticked-off banshee, a "pesky" intestinal imbalance and an actual FBI rap sheet.

And there's the rub. Thanks to the federal Hurt Feelings police at the Fair Housing Authority, you're hamstrung. You can no longer offer intelligent, helpful, informative answers to your tenants' questions.

Did you know that you can no longer refer to a large closet as a "walk-in" closet? Yep. According to the federal frumps at Fair Housing, if word ever got out that somebody somewhere had walked into a closet, then somebody somewhere else - somebody that has trouble walking, maybe - might get their feelings hurt. (Of course, people come *out* of closets all the time, although "walking" might be too pedestrian a term for the activity. But Closet Liberation Theology is handled by an entirely different federal department.)

Nor can you refer to your property as "within walking distance to the mall." See, in the federal government, they think so little of us that they've convinced themselves that we'll never make it without their manic nanny-like oversight. And their only solution, their only reaction, is to over-react: not every single human can walk, so let's just not mention walking, and then maybe walking will just go away.

I don't know *how* walking will go away, because, well, walking went away, right? But there's an entirely different federal department handling that. (It used to be NASA that handled such time-travel conundrums, but NASA now has the operational budget of a nine-year-old's lemonade stand, only with less pending lawsuits.)

It gets more weird. That largest bedroom in each apartment? You know, the one with the, um...the, uh...the drive-in closet? You can no longer refer to that room as the "master" bedroom. (However, there are specific IRS exemptions available if you are a gainfully employed Argentine Dogo rooming with your master, who happens to be an NFL quarterback.)

Next to be outlawed, I suppose, will be any references to the <gasp!> sitting room. Not everybody can just sit whenever they bloody well care to sit, you know. Especially if you're one of those enterprising apartment communities in the Rust Belt, pulling in a little extra coin by running a meth lab in the on-site Laundromat.

So, to help you fine-tune your telephony skills, here's yet another helpful quiz.

A prospect calls with a question about closet space. The federal Hurt Feelings police won't let you say "walk-in closet." How do you respond?

a)   All our closets are walk-in closets. You just can't walk in very far.

b)   Our bedrooms boast monstrous closets, once you get shoved in there. Ask about our personalized shoving service!

c) I don't know from "walk-in," but we once offered run-in closets. Made an absolute killing on forfeited security deposits.

While researching your competition, their saleswoman quotes this phrase from their marketing brochure: "Many residents have large dogs or alarms that will automatically call the police department." How do you respond?

a) Just pure coincidence, I guess, that you guys are running that "secret" meth lab in the Laundromat?

b) If your place is anything like my place, calling the police department is a briskly optimistic exercise.

c) Cool! Where can I get me one o' them phone-dialing dogs?

A prospect calls with a question about bedrooms. The federal Hurt Feelings police won't let you mention "master" bedroom. How do you respond?

a) All our units feature a humorously small bedroom and a ridiculously small bedroom. Legend has it that, once upon a time, someone almost slept in the "humor suite," but we can't confirm that.

b) The standard floor plan offers three sleeping cells; one dominant and two submissive. Were you interested in something more bitter?

c) Be sure to ask about our Simon Legree discount!

What is the proper way to answer a Customer Service phone call?

a) Hi, my name is Ted. Can I help you?

b) Hi, I'm Ted. I can help you.

c) Hi, I'm Ted, and if I can help you, nobody will be more surprised than me.

A prospect is interested in your apartment and asks about proximity to grocery stores. The federal Hurt Feelings police won't allow you to use the expression "within walking distance." How do you respond?

a) There are several grocery stores within alking-way istance-day.

b) Several grocery stores are unbelievably close, if you happen to have eight surface-gripping appendages!

c) Hey, I remember you! I took you to lunch, and you ate lunch *twice, in my car, on the way to lunch.* I need to hook you up with Kip, the guy who runs our Laundromat.

A tenant with a question about "maximum occupancy" calls to ask, "Somehow, I got pregnant. At what age do you recognize children?" How do you respond?

a) For the purposes of occupancy, we recognize children at birth.

b) For the purposes of occupancy, we recognize children at age two.

c) Somehow, ma'am? *Somehow* you got pregnant? Any idea who the mother is?

A prospect is interested in your apartment and asks for directions to the property. The federal Hurt Feelings Police won't allow you to mention the obvious landmark, that massive twenty-four-acre Protestant church on the corner. How do you respond?

a) Go three miles on Main, then turn left at the big pointy building.

b) Go four miles on Main, turn around, go back one mile, then turn right.

c) Drive down Main Street until you come to the only intersection within fifty-miles that doesn't have a pharmacy on the corner. Turn left.

A tenant calls with a question about their garage. How do you qualify their question?

a) If the garage is attached, ask the caller for the apartment number.

b) If the garage is detached, ask the caller for the garage number.

c) If the garage is not detached but just reticent, or a bit aloof, ask to speak to an adult garage.

So, there you are, citizens. Don't be idle! Get out there, find your litigious niche, and start getting sued for something!

If you have any other questions, feel free to come see us at El Permanente Los Wages Garden Estates At Blynken West, Phase IV. Just head down Broad Street and turn left at the First United Methodi...uh...just hang a left at the first intersection that has fabulous landscaping, no satellite dish, and a tax-exempt status.

No appointment necessary! Just walk right in and...um...ah...

Just, uh...just...

Please call to make an appointment.

Full Frontal Stupidity

Abby Redux VIII

(Our favorite grumpy columnist finally meets her neighbors)

This week, the hottest news stories in America are
1. The Super Bowl
2. The Presidential campaign
3. Various people butchering the National Anthem

(Oddly enough, all of these topics involve Roseanne Barr. Well, not all at once.)

So, naturally, given these world-shaping stories that are competing for everyone's attention, I'm going to address the obvious burning topic:

Apartment maintenance.

And we'll let Abby handle the butchering.

Now, for those of you who haven't met her, Abby Redux is an advice columnist who drops by from time to time. Abby has several interesting characteristics:

1.   She has the same first name as another famous advice columnist
2.   She has a very bad attitude, an extremely cynical demeanor, and no patience whatsoever
3.   She doesn't actually exist

(Oddly enough, neither does Rosanne Barr. Well, not all at once.)

Normally, Abby fields questions about life, love, and relationships, and then helpfully lobs back scathing insults. But this week, things got weird, as things sometimes will, especially when you're making them up. This week, we've got her handling emails - maintenance requests (yes, they're real) from residents (no, they're not real) at Abby's apartment community, Belle Leigh Acres. (also not real, but it should be)

And if you think there's a whole lot of unreality going on *here*, you should see the Presidential campaign...

~-~-~-~-~-~

Dear Abby Redux,
The vent keeps running and won't turn off.
Signed, Tony

Dear Tony,
Don't worry about it. But please let us know if the light starts sucking air out of the room.

~-~-~-~-~-~

Dear Abby Redux,
The toilet runs inside itself.
Signed, Rey

Dear Rey,
We'll get you a more outgoing toilet.
~-~-~-~-~-~

Dear Abby Redux,
The heater will not turn on at all, and when it does, it won't blow hot air.
Signed, Marla

Dear Marla,
Won't turn on at all, eh? Except when it does, huh? Okay, here's the plan. We won't come fix it, but when we do, we won't not fix it. At all.
~-~-~-~-~-~

Dear Abby Redux,
The fridge light is out again.
Signed, Unit 311

Dear 311,
Remember, earlier this year? Our little "plugging in the appliances" tutorial? Remember?
~-~-~-~-~-~

Dear Abby Redux,
The disposal has started smoking.

Signed, Hubert

Dear Hubert,
You should see *my* place. The microwave has started drinking, the Panini machine's playing poker till all hours, and the vanity mirror's addicted to vampire novels.
~-~-~-~-~-~-~

Dear Abby Redux,
The towel rack in 114 needs a drywall nil.
Signed, Call Center

Dear Call Center,
We'll be sure to not do anything.
~-~-~-~-~-~-~

Dear Abby Redux,
The fridge light is out again.
Signed, Unit 311

Dear 311,
We'll fix it again. In the meantime, shine the vent on it.
~-~-~-~-~-~-~

Dear Abby Redux,
The garbage disposal doesn't work. It hasn't worked since John moved in.
Signed, Call Center

Dear Call Center,
Please have John stop living under the sink. Obviously, he rusts.

~-~-~-~-~-~

Dear Abby Redux,
The kitchen lights are leaking.
Signed, Andrea

Dear Andrea,
Do you know Tony, the guy with the running vent?
~-~-~-~-~-~

Dear Abby Redux,
The widow in the master bedroom is cracked.
Signed, Bruce

Dear Bruce,
That's *your* opinion. Listen, there's a guy down the hall who lives under his sink.
~-~-~-~-~-~

Dear Abby Redux,
The tenant fell and put a hole in the wall.
Signed, Call Center

Dear Call Center,
The landlord will send condolences and then put a hole in the tenant's deposit.
~-~-~-~-~-~

Dear Abby Redux,
The fridge light is out again. This has happened before.
Signed, Unit 311

Dear 311,
Happened before what?

~-~-~-~-~-~

Dear Abby Redux,
Please remove the hair from the guest bathroom, which belonged to the previous owner.
Signed, Anna

Dear Anna,
Well, of *course* the bathroom belonged to the previous owner. The hair, though? That could be anybody's. I suggest you shower at the Y.

~-~-~-~-~-~

Dear Abby Redux,
There's a dead frog or mouse in the third bedroom.
Signed, Kamir

Dear Kamir,
I'm gonna need to know if it's a frog or a mouse. We're a Union shop.

~-~-~-~-~-~

Dear Abby Redux,
The washer damaged our trowels.
Signed, Tom & Lisa

Dear T&L,

Yeah, when it comes to shovels, washing machines can be a bit finicky. You might want to look into going outside to hose down your garden tools. Have you buffet-slayers considered eating with forks, like normal-sized people?
~-~-~-~-~-~

Dear Abby Redux,
The ice maker needs to be checked to see if it is working in the off position.
Signed, Joe

Dear Joe,
I'm gonna go out on a limb here - you've never been a returning 'Jeopardy' champion, have you, Joe?
~-~-~-~-~-~

Dear Abby Redux,
There is a wet spot in the living room floor that is wet.
Signed, Cissy

Dear Cissy,
Shut up.
~-~-~-~-~-~

Dear Abby Redux,
The AC is leaking through the wall. The resident stated that this happened last summer.
Signed, Call Center

Dear Call Center,

It happened last summer, and *now* they're whining? Tell them to review the 'Statutes of Limitations' section in our Resident Manual. Tell them to review it last summer.

~-~-~-~-~-~

Dear Abby Redux,
The dishwasher leaks when in use from the bottom.
Signed, Sid

Dear Sid,
Yeah, I would think it might.

~-~-~-~-~-~

Dear Abby Redux,
There appears to be a wet spot on the left as you come in. The carpet stays wet. There is a dog in the home.
Signed, Call Center

Dear Call Center,
Shoot the dog. If you think it'll help, shoot the carpet, too.

~-~-~-~-~-~

Dear Abby Redux,
This is a 2nd request. The first request was pickled up by maintenance.
Signed, Freddie

Dear Freddie,
Odd that you should choose the word "pickled." Wait till you see our night watchman.

~-~-~-~-~-~

Dear Abby Redux,
The bathroom fan in 240 is not working. She would like Jose to do in.
Signed, Call Center

Dear Call Center,
Yeah, I just bet she would.
~-~-~-~-~-~

Dear Abby Redux,
I have ants in my kitchen. Come any time, I only have a cat.
Signed, Antonio

Dear Antonio,
So you have ants *and* a cat. You, sir, are in serious violation of our pet policy.
~-~-~-~-~-~

Dear Abby Redux,
Over half the home is without power. Please wear booties.
Signed, Tammy in 5-D

Dear Tammy,
Sorry, it's Jose's night to wear the booties.
~-~-~-~-~-~

Dear Abby Redux,
The smoke alarm was going off for no reason and they smell a burning odor.
Signed, Call Center

Dear Call Center,
Mmm hmm. So, what part of 'for no reason' stumped you guys?
~-~-~-~-~-~

Dear Abby Redux,
The outside lights in the common areas are all out inside the building.
Signed, LeeAnn

Dear LeeAnn,
Let me guess, sweetheart. English is a second language.
~-~-~-~-~-~

Dear Abby Redux,
Refrigerator is smoking in back.
Signed, Mary

Dear Mary,
Another fridge hittin' the pipe, eh? Okay, hang on, I'll contact Chilled Protective Services. We've got to nip these things in the bud.
By the way, you didn't see my Panini machine out there, did you?
~-~-~-~-~-~

Dear Abby Redux,
The resident's head is not coming on.
Signed, Call Center

Neither is yours, Call Center.
Neither is yours.

The Good, the Bad, & the Profile-Challenged

(Don't say "ugly." Say "homely-enabled." Or "Jerry Springer guest-ish.")

For the few dozen of you out there who still have a private sector job, I have some breaking news for you. Monday morning, when you get to work, tread lightly. That voracious varmint known as "Political Correctness?" You know, the beast that cannot be fed? It's extended its reach.

It now protects ugly people.

That's right, America. From a legal perspective, ugly people are now a protected class, with their own set of exemptions and extra rights, much like atheists, or Wisconsin schoolteachers. We now have a whole new group of potential workplace-lawsuit victims, whining for advocacy and access, clamoring for attention and attorneys, despite sporting heads that look like they must've lost a bet.

Full Frontal Stupidity

According to this week's cadre of pesky, know-it-all progressive crusaders, discriminating against ugly people in the workforce has suddenly become a huge problem. Personally, I fail to see any evidence of these alleged encroaching tentacles of anti-ugly bigots, if you catch my drift. Ugly's kind of like Sarah Palin, or car commercials: ugly is everywhere. For example, I order fast food almost every day from people who look like they're running late for a Michael Jackson zombie video.

And on behalf of us single guys in the workplace, let me say for the record that we don't need this extra hassle. We had enough hassles already, thank you very much. It's tough enough as it is now, just trying to deal with women and overly-caffeinated sales people. Not to mention grandparents armed with photos.

Sales people are easy. Just tell them they're ugly, and they'll laugh and go away. Long ago, perhaps in utero, they convinced themselves that they're not ugly, because...well...because they're sales professionals!

Alternatively, you could try just killing sales people, but let's be honest - who walks around work all day , handily packing garlic and a stake? Besides, there's no guarantee a sales person will stay dead, especially if they've not yet hit quota.

Women, on the other hand, can be a bit trickier. At work, women immediately outflank guys tactically, for two very good reasons:
1) Women think most guys are idiots
2) Most guys are idiots

However, women have inherent advantages that further compound the problem:

1) Women have great big eyes. Two, generally.
2) Women have angles and bumps that guys don't have. Well, most guys.
3) Most guys are idiots

And finally, we have grandparents. Grandchild-picture-packing grandparents, when unmonitored and released in a work environment, are ruthless, political and adhesive.

Now, I'm the first to admit that two-week-old babies, as a non-invasive caucus, are ridiculously cute, and they stay cute until there are mitigating factors, like decorative body piercings, or proms, or pending indictments.

But two-*minute*-olds? No. Sorry, no. Extremely newborns look like Mr. Magoo would look after getting his hand caught in a vise.

But grandparents don't see it that way. They have a bias, and they're on a mission. Somehow, at the hospital, they'd managed to smuggle a camera into Labor & Delivery and then snap candid photos of their own child's child, a tiny, damp, six-second-old future human who doesn't even have a fig leaf or a Facebook account. I mean, here's a hapless, naked little biped who as yet hasn't even worked out that whole inhale/exhale thing. The poor, wailing congealed kid looks like a mini-Bill Murray, just off of a "Ghostbusters" slime outtake.

To a grandparent, however, this little bundle is the galaxy's first perfected person. Until now, every other human was just a flawed draft.

To a grandparent, this child is the apex of history's vast sweep, the acme of personhood.

To your average guy on his morning break, it's a grainy Mutual of Omaha marginally-viable prairie mammal.

So, be warned. It's just a matter of time before some grandparent corners you at work and proudly whips out snaps of the former fetus (undoubtedly saddled with a name like William Overlord Johnson III, a name that weighs more than the kid itself). There's no graceful way to deal with this tricky social challenge, other than the obvious, time-tested, manly solution:

Lie.

Yes, lie. Lie like lying was an Olympic event. Lie like lying is a newly-unearthed Commandment. And don't look at me like that. As if you're offended or something.

You're not fooling anybody, you know. You've lied twice since you started reading this. You lied to *get* this job.

I mean, what are you gonna say to the grandguy as he proudly brandishes progeny-once-removed? The truth?

1)   Holy rainwater! What morphing software are you using?
2)   Isn't that the two-nosed alien Han Solo blasted in the *Star Wars* bar?

3) None of my business, of course, but why are you carrying around a photo of Jonathan Winters in a hurricane?

I rest my case.

So let's review some scenarios. Ready?

Because you were distracted, Tony from Accounting (a new grandparent) managed to corner you at the water cooler. As you calculate sprinting distances to the various exits, Tony rakes your cheek with a photo and launches a salvo:

Scenario 1: Grandpa Tony says, "Is that not the most handsomest child you ever saw?"

Your optimal response?
    a) Tony, I've never seen a more beautiful baby in my life!
    b) Whoa! What, did somebody dip the kid in something?
    c) Aw, Tony, he looks just like you, if you were Mr. Magoo and had been in a serious shop accident!

Scenario 2: Grandpa Tony says, "Look at that grin, eh? This one's gonna be a handful!"

Your optimal response?
    a) Yep, trouble for sure, that one! Heh heh.
    b) Tony, that's not his grin. Somebody flip the kid.
    c) Well, whaddaya know! I didn't realize recidivism was an acquired trait.

So be careful, worker guy. Remember, ugly people are out there, and now they can sue you. Now they're a protected class. An endangered species, even. Maybe. Hopefully.

Ugly, in solidarity.

I just hope they're still a minority.

Table for One?

(Why we need a cost-of-living index for Single Guys)

A friend came to work this week with a tin of excellent homemade cookies. Cinnamon-topped, crunchy around the edges, chewy in the middle. I don't know if the entire batch was dependable, but the twenty-nine I ate were top-shelf.

I fondly filed the memory away as, well, cinnamon cookies. But it turned out that these cookies were a commonly shared confection, with a name well-known to parents and other humans who drive SAVs. ("Suburban Assault Vehicles" - you know, those two-story cars-on-steroids that sport warehouse-sized sliding doors, theatre seating, and a gas tank the size of Lake Mead.)

And it also turned out that I was the only guy in the room who didn't know that this tasty little cookie is a common snack, commonly called a "Snickerdoodle."

Snickerdoodle: the familiar name of this cinnamon cookie I was eating (and the one I was about to eat, and the three or four I ate already, and the half-dozen I'd hidden under paper towels, a legal pad and various opaque desk ornaments).

Now. For the record: at the time, earlier, when my friend had offered me a cookie, I do remember him saying something like, "yep, the wife makes excellent Snickerdoodles." But at the time, I shook that comment off as irrelevant. TMI. It was way early in the morning, I hadn't had any coffee, and I didn't really care to hear about anybody's sex life.

And so it goes for single guys. We're used to it, but so it goes. There's a whole sub-culture out there, privy to information to which single guys are rarely exposed. On the other hand, single guys have access to tons of handy little factoids that would probably seem inexplicable to Great Dads Throughout History -- iconic symbols of parenting, like Ward Cleaver. Homer Simpson. Ozzy Osbourne. Catherine the Great's horse.

Partly, I suppose, it's a matter of perspective. Single guys often see things differently, or miss things entirely, or sometimes see things that remain unseen to married bipeds and other humans who are, shall we say, less commitment-challenged.

Here's an example. Most of you family-types out there buy milk in enormous containers called "gallons." Single guys buy milk in small, manageable doses known as "pints," as if they were bringing home beer, or morals. It would never cross a single guy's mind to bring home an entire gallon of *anything*, much less some consumable breakfast liquid that can mutate into something that smells like downtown Detroit looks.

Here's another example of Single Guy perspective. I had been out of college for nearly a decade before I learned that shower curtains are replaceable. Single guys just assume that, as part of life's rich pageantry, we're given one shower curtain each, and that's our quota. Unless, of course, somebody steals it, or it gets used in any activity that involves Catherine the Great's horse.

Right about now, you may be thinking, "Well, that's just stupid. Of *course* you can replace a shower curtain! Otherwise, the thing just gets more and more disgusting, what with all the mildew, pizza stains, and hoof prints."

Pizza stains? *Pizza stains?* And you're questioning *my* commentary?

Of course, to be fair to the Single Guy Nation, not all single guys are as stupid as I. Or as stupid as me. Or equally unsmart like I or me am or are. I hope you get my point, because I forgot what I was talking about.

Oh, yeah. Cookies.

According to one recipe I found on the internet, you'll not get far as a Snickerdoodle Maven without having various accesses to various amounts of various products, including shortening, sugar, eggs, flour, cream of Tartar, baking soda, salt and cinnamon.

I checked my own pantry. (First, I had to ring up my wicked step-ex-girlfriend, Emasculata, to find out where it was.) You know how many of those Snickerdoodle-enabling ingredients I own?

Salt.

(Actually, I did find some cinnamon, but it was in a dust-creased jar bearing a cheesy "As seen on *'Bewitched!'*" promo and a label that warned, "Best if used by the Tet Offensive.")

And should I ever run out of Tartar cream, I wouldn't even know where to start. What aisle at the grocery stocks pre-Mongol Turkic ethnic groups? Can I get just the cream, sold in a tube, or a jar, or a goatskin? Or do you have to buy the whole Tartar, get the guy home, and then employ some ancient Tartar-cream-separating Iranian farm implement? Do Tartars expire?

Eggs, for a single guy, fall into the same category as milk. Basically, the problem is this - the stuff spoils. It goes bad, and quickly, too, like Rod Stewart trying to sing "It Had To Be You."

(This short-term temporal window also holds true for bags of lettuce, very expensive cheese, and very cheap pork.)

Such grocer's purchases present an insurmountable container-to-consumer ratio. It's just math. The stuff simply can't be swallowed, by one person, prior to the expiration date. A single guy ends up dashing about, looking for stuff to throw milk on, or at, or in.

(Consumer Tip: There is no food item that, having been handed to you via a car window, will get better by being dipped in nearly expired milk. None. There just isn't.)

(Humane Tip: Leaving several unattended bowls of milk in one's front yard, in hopes of conscripting cats to consume the stuff, may lead to unexpected side-effects. Cats tend to view such largesse as the onset of a "trend." This is closely followed by a "social contract" and, ultimately, an "entitlement.")

Fortunately, eggs have alternative uses, including deliciously violent functions that involve safe, healthy playground concepts like arc, carpet-bombing, trajectory, splatability, and so on.

And shortening? I don't even know what shortening is, other than a dim childhood memory ("*Mama's little baby loves shortenin' bread*") from some song that I don't think we're supposed to sing anymore.

(Later on in the song, some single guy apparently does something stupid in the kitchen with the shortenin' bread lady, and it costs him a year in jail, where he learns many new vocabulary words, like "recidivism" and "shiv." Meanwhile, upstairs in this doomed household, some bed-sick kids smell the bread, get out of bed, and attack a pigeon, for some shortening-induced reason. The place was out of control.)

Come to think of it, maybe it's better if we *don't* sing that song anymore.

Rites & Recidivism (Holidays & History)

~*~*~

"I am not young enough to know everything."

Oscar Wilde

~*~*~*~*~

Full Frontal Stupidity

Today Only - 77 Trombones!

(One small step for man; one giant weekend tent sale!)

July 4, 1776. I can hear it now. Thomas Jefferson's famous prophecy of patriotism: "My fellow citizens, this is the day. Throughout America's future, this sacred day will stand apart from all others as the day when we celebrate our hard-fought freedom by offering deep discounts on fitted sheets."

America. Land of the free shipping and home of "The Brave Wear Briefs" Three-Day Sale.

I don't know where you spent your Fourth of July holiday weekend, but wherever you were, it couldn't have been crowded, because everybody in America was with me. Somehow, this holiday Saturday, roughly twenty-seven million Americans managed to discover what errands I had to run, what items I needed to buy, and from where, and then they all managed to beat me there. Every single one of 'em. Driving like Otis from Mayberry, parking like Salvador Dali, bouncing from aisle to aisle like Arlen Specter, and charging like a hippopotamus might

115

charge if a hippopotamus could run for Congress and spend other people's money, and besides, hippos would probably be less cocky, and definitely better behaved. (I don't know if hippos have morals, but then ... yeah, you know where this is going.)

My first stop, the grocery, was a chaos, something along the lines of 1975 Saigon during "last call." Soft drinks were being traded as commodities, chips and dips were a faded memory, and cookout buns were as rare as leftover money at a Pentagon budget summit. Even in the Four-Hundred-Thousand Items Or Less lane, sympathetic staff were doling out cots and complimentary shampoo. And I'm not sure, but based on observed buying patterns, I believe some shoppers had been told that spare ribs could cure cancer.

But this is what we've done to ourselves. We celebrate with sales. We consecrate with cash or credit, we honor with outlay, we praise with "paper or plastic?" Whether it's Christmas, Thanksgiving, President's Day, Spam & Three-Bean Milkshake Day, National Midget Aardvark Preservation Week, the Cinco of Mayo, or The Fourth of July, car dealers and other one-celled organisms will find a way to turn a holiday into a way to turn a dollar.

And this Independence Day weekend was no different. Every surviving, un-shuttered shop with a shingle and a shill had some barbed "Buy here if you love America" lure, spinning on some lame marketing hook, feebly tied to the "theme" of the national holiday. Used cars for $1776, that sort of nonsense.

A local clothing store teased that any second item was only $76. For a loss leader, the grocery led with thirteen-to-a-dozen "Original Colony Eggs," and a fast food joint was hawking Cornwallis dogs with a side of Cheez Yankee Doodles. An uncommonly large, muumuu-ed woman named Estelle took out a half-page newspaper ad touting a special group therapy session, billing it as Codependence Day. ("Girl, we didn't need the British, and you don't need him!")

A regional weight loss center named Heft Hiders unveiled a new "Give me 76 sit-ups or give me death" exercise plan, an over-eager orthodontist marketed his "1812 Overbite," and an obviously holiday-challenged entrepreneur was pushing Rosa Parks' memorial seat cushions. An appliance store promotion promised a free "Philadelphia Flier" dryer with the purchase of any new "Washing-ton" machine, but thankfully, a hole suddenly ripped opened in the Universe and the store's marketing department was sucked away to that dark place were really bad puns go to die.

Cell phone companies promised steep discounts on all phone calls, as long as the calls were made within one of the thirteen original colonies, lasted exactly 76 minutes, and were completed prior to the end of the Spanish-American war. (Some ante-bellum connection charges may apply. Offer not valid in New Jersey, North America, or Earth.)

And of course, in Washington, you could get a sweet deal on an overnighter in the Lincoln Bedroom.

Meanwhile, the home improvement stores were particularly frenzied this year, given the current state of our housing market. (see "Saigon 1975") You know these stores, or at least the two major competitors. I forget their names; Home Skillet and Low Depot, maybe, something like that. One is orange, the other is blue.

For a marketing slogan, one of the two, the blue or the orange, I forget which, was inviting shoppers to swing round and "build something together, that will utterly void your warranty," while the other was pumping up Joey Homeowner's ego with the reassuring jingle, "You can do it. Maybe. Okay, probably not. We can help, though we might or might not, depending."

I forget which store is the reassuring one, but the other one, the codependent one, might want to consider brokering a cooperative marketing venture with Estelle.

Both stores have parking lots the size of some small European nations, and they're both populated by roving, color-coordinated-vest-wearing squadrons of savants who all somehow manage to know everything there is to know about lumber, toilets, lawns, lawnmowers, grills, shelving, paint, brushes, blinds, boring tools, bits, brads, nails and anodized self-tapping chrome-plated toilet brush gasket caps.

And these cavernous competitors are always located right across the street from each other. I suppose there are hordes of insecure shoppers out there right now, constantly zipping back and forth across the divider highway, looking for the three-penny-better bargain on cap-tapping chrome-gasketed anodyne brush-mounted free-range toilet air-gun self-dissolving pre-greased flag mounts.

"Let's build something together," they say. This Saturday, apparently, the something they were planning to build together was an epic, eight-lane, cross-country mulch highway, laid down by an army of buffet-enabled workers boldly outfitted in the most horrid plaid shorts imaginable.

Visiting the blue and orange giants always reminds me of a line by the late, brilliant comedian, Mitch Hedberg:

"I don't own a house. I rent an apartment. People like me need a store called 'Apartment Depot' - a great big huge store, full of people just hangin' out, saying, 'We ain't gotta fix *nuthin*'."

So. Happy Independence Day, America. Now get out there and buy something ... else, the terrorists win.

And let's end the holiday on a happy note: fortunately, neither the orange place nor the blue place is one of those pesky membership clubs. I'm not paying a store *before* I buy something; I'm not paying somebody for the privilege of paying somebody. I have a relationship with my wallet that's far too codependent for anything like *that*.

At least, that's what Estelle told us.

Uncommon Sense

(A competency quiz for Baby Boomers)

My generation's in trouble.

I don't mean in trouble with the law, or anything so dramatic as that. We already went through *that* phase, back in "the day," and we quickly got over the "glamor" of getting arrested.

Admittedly, we were maniacs. We played outside ... OUTSIDE! (though not in our school clothes) We rode bikes, *without helmets*, and didn't die. We played tag, and dodge-ball, and threw rocks, and didn't die. So we might have been rash, at times. But we weren't stupid.

And that's my point. We used to be smart. Because we used to have to remember stuff, like Presidents, and state capitals, and our phone number. Remembering to change out of our school clothes, and not to slam the screen door. Remembering how to play, and dodge rocks, and win, and lose. And not die.

But then we grew up. (Well, many of us grew up. Well, some of us. Okay, you.) And at some point we ceded control. Now, we get all our knowledge from Google, and all our truth from snopes.com.

Now, we don't have to remember anything. We just hop online, google it, verify it, use it, and forget it.

And now look at us Boomers. We're as ignorant as a Senator at an ethics hearing - and as insecure as an éclair at a Paula Deen picnic.

We're the first generation who would ever *dream* of taking the time to reply to an opinion survey with the response 'no opinion.' And *forget* naming the fifty state capitals - without a computer, we can't name fifty *numbers*. (But we don't have to. There's an app for that.)

So, in hopes of helping exercise atrophied craniums everywhere, we've cobbled together this handy Common Sense Quiz. It's guaranteed to be completely fraudulent; however, it's staggeringly useless. (this has been confirmed by snopes.com)

Ready? Let's begin.

~~~~~~~~~

What's the most abundant metal in the Earth's core?
- Aluminum
- Dirt
- Led Zeppelin

Can you name three of the original states?

- Maryland, Virginia and Conneti ... Cunect ... Kinnec ... Georgia
- Maryland, Clemson and Boston College
- No

If you rearranged the letters "PZOMKSLA" you would have

- the name of an animal
- the name of a country
- the name of an Eastern European hockey player
- wasted several minutes

A farmer has thirteen cows. A bolt of lightning kills all but five of them. How many cows survived?

- Eight
- Five
- None. The farmer also kept zoo animals. Then one day, he went insane, released them, and they ate all the cows.

ESSAY QUESTION: Mary, who is sixteen years old, is four times as old as her brother, who likes to wear Mary's clothes. How old will Mary be when her brother is eligible for early parole?

Why are there 100 Senators in the Senate?

- The Constitution provides for two Senators from each state.
- The Founding Fathers only budgeted for 100 chairs.

- In my entire life, I have *never* seen 100 Senators in the Senate, and neither have you.

Complete the following sentence: When faced with unexpected events, _____
- I know I can rise to the challenge.
- I wonder if I can cope.
- I buckle like the fender on an electric car.

What do you put in a toaster?
- Toast
- Bread
- Barry Manilow CDs

Which one of the four is least like the other three?
- Dog
- Coyote
- Wolf
- John Edwards

Who presides over your local government?
- My County Commissioners
- My Mayor and community council
- My cousin's stepfather, Big Tony

Which one of the four is least like the other three?
- Canine
- Incisor
- Molar

- John Edwards

ESSAY QUESTION: A friend you believed to be close suddenly breaks off all communication for no apparent reason. You leave phone messages but get no reply. How long do you wait before de-friending her, updating your Facebook status, and flaming her reputation?

In terms of keeping appointments, I am likely to arrive
- Slightly early
- Slightly late
- Yes, I am.

What kinds of words are used in the following sentences: "Wow! My grandpa did a backflip!"
- Two nouns, one verb, and an interjection
- An action, a reaction and an injunction
- Lies

Sally has three coins equaling fifty-five cents. One of the coins is not a nickel. What are the three coins?
- Two quarters and a nickel.
- One half-dollar and two very strange pennies.
- Someone else's. Sally is a kleptomaniac.

For what chemical process do plants need sunlight, carbon dioxide, and water?
- Photojournalism
- Precipitation
- Plant sex

ESSAY QUESTION: You're driving a bus from Jacksonville to Miami. At St. Augustine, 11 people get on the bus. At Daytona, 3 riders get off and 9 get on. In Boca Raton, 4 more passengers climb on and 3 exit the bus. How many passengers will make it all the way to Miami if the toothless guy in the back wearing the choir robe and fur hat keeps arguing with the luggage rack?

"Acquiesce" is the opposite of
- Agree
- Disagree
- Quiesce

Who elects the President of the United States?
- The electoral college
- The citizens of the United States
- An evil international banking consortium that would flick you off this planet like a limp mouse carcass

Complete the following sentence: I did _____ on my grammar test.
- good
- well
- not cheat much
- a backflip

What is the introduction to the Constitution called?
- The Pre-Ramble
- The Disclaimer
- The Acquiescence

ESSAY QUESTION: Johnny needs seventeen bottles of water from the store. Johnny can only carry three bottles of water at a time. What do you suppose is going on at Johnny's house that requires all that water?

During a morning break at work, I usually take the opportunity to
- Chat with my coworkers
- Have some time to myself
- Cart off some more office supplies
- Detox

Complete the following sentence: As a rule, politicians should be _____.
- in favor of term limits
- inspired by a humble, public-serving nature
- indicted

Jack had two rabbits. Then his mom gave him a turtle and another rabbit. How many rabbits does Jack have now?
- Counting the turtle?
- Could be dozens. You know how rabbits can be when it comes to photojournalism. They're worse than plants. Or John Edwards.
- Two. He swapped the new one for fifty-five cents with Sally.

~~~~~~~~~

So, how'd you do? Feeling smarter already, aren't you? Excellent!

And now, where do we go from here?

I have no clue.

Google it.

Fang Festival Follies

(Kids. Candy. Corpses. Career politicians. Okay, no corpses.)

Well, here in my neighborhood, we've all managed to survive yet another pagan-based festival. You know the occasion - the one where diminutive, oddly-dressed strangers coalesce in the twilight to gang-beg you and your neighbors. They materialize at your door, they rap or ring, they all chant the same, tired, terse half-promise-half-threat mantras, and they blithely demand you hand over some valuables to support their cause.

That's right. It's that Fall favorite - the political election season.

I'm kidding, of course. Sorta. The festival at hand is what we Americans now call Halloween. It's had other names. All Hallowmas. The Day of the Dead. Feralia. All Hallows Eve. All Saints Day. Guy Fawkes Day. (By the way, you can thank Guy Fawkes for dragging politics into Halloween, thereby ruining a perfectly good holiday where America's kids get to celebrate evil undead things AND tooth decay.)

129

Depending on your research sources, Halloween was invented long ago, either thanks to British pagans, or in spite of ancient Romans, or because of Bailey's Irish Cream, or by Al Gore. Two thousand years ago, according to one story, the Boston Celts celebrated year's end on October 31 (their fiscal year began in November, for tax purposes). They called this year-end festival "Samhain," partly because nobody could say "Auld Lang Syne" without snickering.

But in a typically stubborn Boston solidarity, they pronounced Samhain like this: "sow-en." In those olden days, that sort of rude, tricky pronunciation was not allowed outside of France. (France was formerly known as "Gall," so named by guests who got their hotel bill.)

Soon, therefore, the Vatican intervened, and Alexander Pope Paul IV McCartney dispatched a cheapmason named Hadrian to England, where Hadrian built a WalMart. (The Pope couldn't find a freemason.) Within minutes, the WalMart advertised a deep discount on candy, which was a pretty good trick, given that it would be another 1,400 years before Johannes Gutenberg invented classified ads.

And the rest is history.

One of Halloween's benefits - and there aren't many - is that the costumes help us gauge who's currently important (or cool) in our culture. In my neighborhood, Spiderman is big, but so are some of the classic bad guys. Dracula always makes the Top Ten list. Frankenstein is popular, but then, in South Carolina, neck bolts qualify as orthodonture. On the other hand, Mao and Pol

Pot are nowhere to be found, although, given their height, they ought to be solid players.

And you almost *never* see a kid dressed up like Guy Fawkes.

(To be fair, however, it takes a special kind of reckless abandon to wear knickers, then and now.)

But now that Halloween has come and gone, I have a question. If Halloween was All Hallows Eve, and the "eve" part has passed, where are all the Hallows? Personally, I've only seen three Dead People, and two of them were WalMart greeters.

Anyway, back to the day itself...about two hours before dark, I ran a quick pre-Halloween quality control test on a Tootsie Roll. Now, the last time I ate a Tootsie Roll was, well, decades ago. Way back. Back before we fully understood the dire threat of sexual harassment in the workplace (or, as we used to say before Political Correctness, "compliments"). I don't think NASA had even driven out to Arizona to fake the moon landing yet.

So my T-Roll memories could be a bit hazy. But this dark, gummy little log I bit into on Halloween was amazingly non-enjoyable (or, as we used to say before Political Correctness, "nasty"). Maybe I'm just too old to appreciate it anymore. Or too tall.

But for pure persistence, you can't beat a Tootsie Roll. Four hours later, I was still chewing the foul thing.

And since Halloween is our topic, let's not forget the little (and not so little) trick-or-treatniks themselves. Witness:

- Just before dark, my first Halloween guest presented. Great mask, this kid. Scary, in a forty-inch-high kind of way. But I couldn't quite grasp his overarching concept, his meta-narrative. He was either a Transformer or a World Series umpire. Or Nancy Pelosi, as viewed before morning coffee.

- The next kid must have sensed that I am "costume-challenged" (or, as we used to say before Political Correctness, "stupid"). This child piped right up and proudly announced himself: "I'm Captain America!" I snapped him a salute and said, "Yes, you are. And you're doing a great job for the country, sir." His eyes widened, he perfected his posture, returned my salute, and gifted me with a smile that could melt glaciers. I think he grew two inches. I think I did, too.

- One kid, I definitely recognized. He wears a Mitt Romney's hair costume, and he's been showing up perennially for over six years. Somehow, the hair has perfect teeth. This year, he took credit for denying that he had taken credit for not having denied anything. Another kid wearing a Rick Perry mask yelled "flip flop," but he misspelled it.

- Another youngster showed up dressed as a Jet Blue pilot. I gave him candy, but I made him wait seven hours for it.

- Just after sunset, a monstrously obese, extremely sweaty kid wearing a Michael Moore mask stormed up to my porch, accused me of having candy, and filmed a documentary of himself eating it. Then he slipped into a sugar coma and repatriated to Cuba, where he died from outstanding medical care.

- A kid wearing a Lindsay Lohan mask didn't show up, repeatedly.

- One shifty-looking truant showed up dressed as Arlen Specter. He had two masks, and knocked on my front and back doors.

- A kid wearing a Sarah Palin mask rang my doorbell. When I offered her candy, she riffled through the basket, dropped to one knee, and field-dressed a Reese's Cup.

- A diminutive future parolee wearing a Timothy Geithner mask rang my doorbell and yelled, "Trick and Treat!"

- A kid wearing a Stephen King mask rang my doorbell and, as I watched, he drafted, wrote and published a 960-page novel.

- About 200 kids costumed as spoiled brats rang my doorbell, said they were the "Occupy Barry" 99%, demanded candy, and started setting up tents on my property. I had them arrested. End of story. No more news here. No film at eleven. (note to self: call Mayor Bloomberg)

- A kid wearing an Eric Holder mask came by and offered me contraband candy. When I accepted it, the kid had me arrested for having contraband candy.

- Down the street, a kid wearing a mask with no face was sexually harassed by a kid costumed as Herman Cain.

- Two kids dressed as Somali pirates stole my doorbell. They tried to ransom it to Greece. (see "stupid")

- A kid wearing a Joe Biden mask rang the doorbell, but we're in mixed company here, so I can't repeat what he said.

- A kid showed up costumed as Kim Kardashian. In the ensuing twenty minutes, we got married, had a whirlwind honeymoon, filmed a reality show, were spotted having a bitter public spat at a trendy oyster bar, divorced, and fielded a cable TV offer for a series about lip stress. She got the house, I got visitation rights with the candy, and every other weekend with one lip.

- A kid in a Cinderella costume walked up to my porch. Suddenly, she was accosted by a kid wearing a Bill Clinton mask, who helped himself to her candy, as a kid costumed as an Arkansas State Trooper stood by. When confronted, the Clinton mask insisted "I did not half-sacks with that woman."

- A kid showed up in a Barack Obama mask. He made me give my candy to the house next door.

And finally, as I gnaw my way through this lingering Tootsie Roll, let's dispense with all the neurotic jabber about Halloween being evil. I don't really believe Halloween is evil. WalMart might be evil. Guy Fawkes, maybe. Tootsie Rolls, definitely. But Halloween? No. Halloween's not evil.

Unless teeth are holy.

All I Want for [Censored]

(Scrooge would've been proud. For a while.)

Christmas. Arguably, the most well-known holiday in the history of history, if you discount that day in 3050 BC when the Arabs invented zero trans-fat, racial profiling, and fruitcake re-gifting.

Okay, not all Arabs were responsible for fruitcake. According to legend, fruitcake was invented by a confectioner named Mischal-Toh, who founded the first-ever Semite bakery, "House Wheat it Is." (Mischal-Toh would later establish the first non-denominational deli-bookstore combo, "To Bialy Or Not To Bialy.")

Admittedly, Christmas is an odd tradition, especially when we try to explain it to children. Reindeer fly. Snowmen live. Strange, strangely-clad, obese, bearded men engage in chimney-oriented home invasions, eat other people's food, and give away stuff, with no regard to any quid pro quo, as if they were fat, hirsute, red-coated liberals.

No wonder kids are confused. Heck, *adults* are confused. I mean, let's face it, adults - getting taller didn't really make us any smarter - it just made us taller. (and our clothes tighter)

But, these days, saying "Christmas" aloud is not allowed, unless you're selling a product so wildly popular that shoppers would swarm in even if you were shrieking "Merry Off-Shore Drilling!"

The only holiday tradition still sacred is the one in which neighbors compete to see who can squeeze 57,500 marginally-yule-related ornaments onto a drab of distressed lawn that's sized to support, at best, six.

What's left? That holiest of holiday icons -- shopping. So, since we can't say Christmas, let's talk about shopping for presents. Here's a list of some of this year's favorites:

~*~*~*~*~*~*

Let's begin our gift list with that government-backed gift albatross that nobody wanted as a gift in the first place - the Electric Car. First of all, thanks to that *other* Santa - the one in the White House - you *already* bought the electric car, you generous taxpayer, you. There's simply no need for you to buy it *again*.

Here's how brilliant the electric car is. It hurls you down the highway at a top speed of ten miles per generation (less if any passengers have facial hair, or there's an oncoming breeze). It'll transport you about forty miles on a dose of electricity, if you've a week to spare.

Here's the little glitch. In the contiguous forty-eight states, there are over 2.9 million miles of paved roads; however, in those same forty-eight states, there are exactly four publicly-available places to recharge your electric car.

But don't sweat it, electric car owner. Soon, there will be, oh, six or seven stations nationally ... unless Congress gets involved, which could result in there being only three, all coincidentally located on the grounds of a tax-exempt country manor owned by the ranking member of a Senate select committee.

It just makes no sense. Only four places to get replacement electricity? I personally know more than four places where I can get a replacement larynx. (Sadly, all four larynx shops are in South Florida - and unlisted - but you can always hitch a ride with some Jersey Shore grandma making a weekend cocaine run. While you're down there, be a tourista: get mauled by a mutant Everglades alligator and take in a snuff film.)

What America really needs is a snap-in device that will de-convert an electric car back to a 1964 Mustang. Or a horse-drawn carriage. Or just a horse. With a horse, the average American could get to the mall *and* deliver the mail.

It makes one wonder why the electric car ever got named the "Volt." Should've been named the "Watt?"
~*~*~*~*~*~*~*

Because the world can never have enough burger-making devices, we now have the "revolutionary" new seven-option griddle from SqueezinArt. After all, nothing says "I love you" like another gift-wrapped slab of dishwasher-safe Teflon.

"Merry Christmas, honey. Here's a flat piece of coated metal that heats up. Lunch ready?"

This culinary breakthrough is a must-have, despite the fact that your pantry floor is already littered with one or more of the previously revolutionary griddles you received in previous holiday seasons:

- The George Foreman griddle, which tenderizes burgers using a patented process known as beating them senseless
- The Black-and-Decker griddle, which not only cooks burgers but also saws the buns in half and constructs a picnic table (patio not included)
- The Hamilton Beach griddle, which we think was named after someone in the Carter administration. It doesn't actually cook burgers, but it lusts after them.

But now, with the revolutionary SqueezinArt griddle, you can cook burgers using the revolutionary "lid open" option, or the revolutionary "lid closed" option, which somehow equals seven options, suggesting that the griddle was designed by the Congressional Budget Office.

~*~*~*~*~*~*~*

Parents of aspiring toddlers will flock to pick up a "My First Genetically Engineered Avian Flu" chemistry set. Imagine the parental pride as your budding chemist learns to comprehend useful vocabulary terms like "pandemic" and "acute toxic kill radius!"

Be sure to stand upwind.

Shopper's Note: the "deluxe" version includes a complimentary "nolo contendere" waiver from Eric Holder's Justice Department and Gun Laundry, as well as a $28 billion R&D coupon from the Pentagon.

~*~*~*~*~*~*~*

For the music-lover on your list, be sure to pick up a copy of the all-new holiday CD, "Yule Hate This," an eclectic collection of carols and chaos brought to you by Largie Small Puff Step-Daddy and those good folks at Angry Goth Zombie Records.

For openers, the unsuspecting listener is subjected to an 18-minute live version of Wu Tang's "Jizzle Bells," followed by Lindsay Lohan doing a cover of "All I Was Wanted For During Christmas." Some forty minutes later, the punishment ends with the Nick Nolte Noel Singers, more-or-less emitting a rousing version of "The Twelve Days Of 500 Bottles Of Christmas Beer On The Wall."

Shopper's Note: Be sure to get your loved ones far, far away before anybody slips this foul thing in the ol' CD player.

~*~*~*~*~*~*~*

Unfortunately, the Snuggie is back this year with a vengeance. Apparently, there's just no avoiding these things. It's like some inescapable, recurrent family curse, or a year-end celebrity news wrap-up from Barbara Walters.

What's infinitely worse is that, like your clever youngster's modified Avian Flu virus, the Snuggie seems to be mutating. We're being invaded by imperfectly-cloned cousins, malformed outfits masquerading as acceptable fashion. There's now something called the Hoodie-Footie, which makes otherwise normal females look like a terry-cloth dishrag, but with eyelashes and breasts.

America, we need to take control of this situation, because, if we're not careful, we could see the re-emergence of velour.

~*~*~*~*~*~*~*

You're going to think I'm insane (if you don't already think I'm insane), but I have to tell you that there is an "Iowa Caucus" iPhone app. There really is. Now you can have instant access to live film footage of Republican Presidential candidates as they carom around both cities in Iowa, documenting their Leader-Of-The-Free-World credentials by getting on a bus, getting off a bus, denying having mocked an opponent's bus in 1968, or getting endorsed by a bus. (fried lard on a stick not included)

I don't mean to be the stormcrow or anything, but I believe this particular omen was mentioned as a "last call" harbinger in the doomsday memoirs of Nostradamus - right there in his Last Days schedule, in-between "city-sucking gaps in the Earth's crust" and "Geraldo Rivera getting a prime-time series."

~*~*~*~*~*~*~*

The hot new interactive game this year is "How to Outwit Airport Security Without Having To Get Naked In Cleveland," v2.1, available for the Wii (by Ninja-Kendo), the Micro$oft X-Box (actual functionality not included), and the Sony Hey-We-Make-Game-Consoles-Too. Unlike previous diversions which catered to familial, multi-player interaction, this year's game is specifically designed for just one participant - just one sad, quiet, lonely, disaffected, bitter participant. Just one jaded juvenile in a jungle-gym crowd.

Just one missed twisted mister, just one more "stunned neighbors who were interviewed recalled a kind, quiet young man" kind of kind, quiet young man. Just one, simple, strong candidate for an "America's Most Wanted" full-hour episode about a seemingly normal, plaid-shorts-wearing, obsessive teeth-grinder.

But enough about Joe Biden.
~*~*~*~*~*~*~*

So, be careful out there, in this holiday traffic, and be sure not to forget the true reason for the season: out-lawn ornamenting your neighbors.

And I hope you have a very Merry ... um ... Wednesday.

Or whatever.

Nibiru, Eris & Fred

(My, how time flies. Has it been 28,000 years already?)

Remember the Y2K scare? When the world ended and everybody died, except people who had a Mac? Remember?

Of course you do. You remember - that ultimate eleventh-hour event that would herald the collapse of civilization, because billions of computers would forget how to add one day to today, as if all the world's laptops had suddenly become Liberal Arts majors.

Entire careers were spawned (or slain) by that Y2K threat, and the worst we got was an anti-climax the size of Bill Gates' divorce settlement.

It was one of those earth-shattering (figuratively) non-events (literally) where everybody got emotionally invested, for zero return. Great huge network teaser, followed by no show. Much ado about much nothing. It was a lot like the over-hyped director's cut of 'Star Wars,' or Bill Clinton playing the sax. (though he still insists he did not have sax)

And now, the doom-mongers are at it again. And, like in 1999, it's a date-based doom. This time, though, they're trying to group-scare us to group-death with an ancient computer - a dysfunctional calendar carved out of stone. Well, nearly carved.

Enter (well, re-enter) the Mayans, a Central American civilization so ancient that they still used Windows XP; a culture so primitive that they signed on as extras in a Mel Gibson movie *without first consulting their agent.* (The film was '*Apocalypto Now*', starring Johnny Depp as Xmzrptlktlotl, and Michael Moore as Central America)

But the Mayan version of Windows (Windows VII BC, codename 'Abattoir') only told us *that* the world would end in late 2012. It didn't tell us *how.* And before anybody could find the instructions, the Mayan's entire operating system crashed, resulting in the first-ever American cultural reboot (literal translation: smallpox).

Fast-forward to today. If we can trust the date as prophesied by the Mayans, the world will likely deep-six itself during one of the 2012 college football post-season bowl games - maybe the Leon Trotsky Yak-Flavored Taco/Sumerian's Revenge Fiesta Dip Bowl - brought to you by those fine folks at Fred's Drive-Thru Parvo Vaccine And Tax Preparation Service, located just off the railway spur in Spine Fungus, Iowa!

"Folks, we'll be right back after this brief commer ... arrgghh."
[extremely bright light]

This would definitely qualify as one of the best - not to mention last - halftime shows *ever*. Total global destruction - now *that's* what I call a 'wardrobe malfunction.'

But here at the corporate headquarters of Don't Worry About It, our advice to you is simple: Don't worry about it. Despite the doomsayers and the 'last chance' car commercials, we're pretty sure that December 21 2012 won't be the end of the world as we know it. It will, however, be another winter solstice. (literal translation: the end of December 21 as we know it)

So, in an effort to calm everybody down, we've assembled a crack team of credentialed scientists, confirmed said credentials (Has unkempt hair; Owns tweed jacket with elbow patches; Has elbows), and asked them to field several of your concerns about 2012 AD, particularly those involving scary predictions and potentially frightening events. (Meteor strike; Mitt Romney getting unkempt hair; Super volcanoes; Rick Perry starring in a remake of 'Hamlet')

~-~-~-~-~-~

Q: Are there any threats to the Earth in 2012?
A: Nothing bad will happen to the Earth in 2012. Our planet has been getting along just fine for more than 4 billion years, and credible scientists worldwide know of no threat associated with 2012. Of course, these are the same scientists who said eggs were good for you.

Q: Is there any danger of Earth being hit by a meteor in 2012?
A: Well, there's always the possibility of impact by a meteor, or a comet, or a rogue Italian cruise ship. But the odds against it are very high, except for the cruise ship. The last big cosmic impact was 65 million years ago, and that led to the extinction of Charles Darwin.

(See *Why you need not fear a supernova before 10:30 AM*)

Q: How do scientists feel about all these claims of pending doomsday?
A: When faced with such queries, the first question out of the mouth of any credible scientist is, "Where is the evidence?" which is why scientists rarely get invited to keg parties. Scientists also have a nasty habit of shoving in footnotes ... worrisome cross-references with the sole purpose of pointing out things that we would've never known we needed to be scared of, had they just kept their mouths shut.

(See *Breathing: what your doctor won't tell you*)

Q: What is the origin of the prediction that the world will end in 2012?
A: There are several such predictions, because, as a global culture, we have pretty much failed at eradicating hophead stupidity. However, one such end-of-all-things story starts with the Sumerians (literal translation: hopheads with sandals), who claimed to have discovered a planet called Nibiru. And supposedly, according to one obscure researcher (Fred Sumerian), Nibiru is barreling toward Earth. Initially, the

catastrophe was predicted for May 2003, but when nothing happened, Fred rescheduled doomsday for December 2012. Obviously, Fred is not well.

Q: Many Internet websites say the world will end in December 2012. Should I be concerned?
A: No. But since you're the type of fringe whack that *believes* those websites, your *coworkers* should be concerned. Most of the internet is garbage, not gospel. Remember, there are also websites for naked biker conventions, for learning how to cheat at Scrabble, and for finding out how to get a government-backed discount mortgage rate if you're an under-aged legally blind female Sumerian vampire in prison.

(See *'The truth about super volcanoes and our penal system'*)

Q: I heard there's a planet called Eris that could collide with Earth this year. Is this true?
A: Eris is a real planet, but it's a dwarf (like Pluto, Thorin Oakenshield, or the measurable value of the UN). Eris would never make it into to the inner solar system, due to planetary physics and intergalactic carry-on baggage restrictions. The closest Eris can come to Earth is about 4 billion miles, which make Eris the perfect place to relocate the UN.

Q: Is there a danger from giant solar storms in 2012?
A: Solar activity has a regular cycle, with peaks approximately every 11 years. To give that some context, the last time there was a giant solar storm, Detroit was still part of the United States, and *Saturday Night Live* was still funny. Usually, the worst thing that can happen during increased solar activity is some

interruption in communications. On the other hand, we could see a rise in lunar activity, which could cause some interruption in Fred.

(See *'Increased lunar activity and heavily-armed library workers'*)

Q: What is the polar shift theory? Is it true that the earth's crust does a 180-degree rotation?
A: A reversal in the rotation of Earth is impossible. (If that happened, cartoons would begin three hours later on the East Coast, and Congress wouldn't stand for it.) However, from time to time, the magnetic polarity of the Earth does reverse. This last happened 400,000 years ago. (It was a Tuesday, about 10:30 in the morning.) As far as we know, such a magnetic reversal wouldn't cause any harm to intelligent life on Earth. (It could, however, doom Congress. This is why, every day at 10:30, Congress goes home and watches cartoons.)

(See *'Polar shift and bipolar vampire health care'*)

Q: Doesn't the Mayan calendar end in December 2012?
A: Yes. As does the calendar on your kitchen wall. And the one in your cube at work. And the one in your boss's office that has 'long golf weekend' scribbled all over it. And that 'Leather-Clad Street-Bike-Riding Chest Mutant of the Month' calendar at the tire store. *All* calendars end, *every* year. See how it works?

Q: Is there really a planet called Nibiru that is approaching Earth and threatening widespread destruction?

A: Look, if Nibiru were real, astronomers would have been all over the story, not to mention Bruce Willis and Roland Emmerich.

Q: But I read that Nibiru could be in disguise, going by the name Eris, or Planet X!
A: Did you now.

Q: By the way, why do you keep qualifying them as 'credible' scientists?
A: Oh, that's an easy one. I have two words for you. Global warming.

(See *'More about Exploding Skin Syndrome'*)

Q: Hey, how about you NASA scientists? What do *you* guys think?
A: Oh, hi, America! Thanks for remembering us! Here at NASA, we're just kind of watching this whole 'doomsday thing' play out ... though we're not getting to watch *much* of it. Thanks to budget cuts, we can now monitor a portion of the cosmos about the size of Rhode Island. (not the state - the hen)

But we'll be fine. Years ago, we started stocking up on MREs and Twinkies. (right after somebody turned us on to Fred's article)

And remember - we invented Tang.

Great Colons in US History

(Never underestimate a Queen & her money)

Columbus Day. That day when we reflect on our national heritage, recall our common status as immigrants, and pay grateful homage to a city in central Ohio.

We all know the story. In 1492, some Italian guy named Chris kept hitting on Isabella, the Queen of Castile. Finally, in an effort to hide from the hormone-infested maniac, Isabella renamed the country "Spain." But Chris still didn't take the hint. So in a last-ditch effort to shake him off, the Queen bought Chris some boats and commissioned him to sail west until he and his ships fell off the edge.

According to the internet, Christopher Columbus was born in 1451, sometime between August 25 and October 31, which is an awfully long time for a woman to be in labor, then or now.

(This may explain why Chris' parents shoved him off to Castile.)

American children know Christopher Columbus as the man who discovered our country, and recognize him from a famous portrait ... some uncomfortable guy, wearing what looks like a limp stealth bomber on his head and a lace Joe Cocker shirt beneath a Spanish Inquisition-era cloak, and nursing the tortured expression of someone with an irritated bowel. In fact, in places where people primarily speak Spanish - places like Spain, California, and most automated telephone systems - Columbus Day is known as "Dia de Cristobal Colon."

An agonized colon. That may explain the Queen's restraint. And the hat.

According to our internet research, our famous little Colon had four brothers. And according to the same research, the four brothers were named Bartolomeo, Giovanni Pellegrino, and Giacomo, and *that*, you'll quickly notice is only three names, and *that*, in our opinion, pretty much sums up internet research.

We can only assume the fourth brother was given a name, possibly il Bastide, or lo Errore, or Son of Latte Delivery Man.

(*And we can only hope that, given his family name, Mama & Papa Colon didn't name the fourth kid Spastic, or Semi.*)

So it's really no surprise that Chris opted to sail away, rather than face an existence flush with missing siblings, snubs by pre-Spanish royalty, and all the inevitable Colon jokes. Plus, Chris had a sneaking suspicion that if he sailed west far enough, he would eventually land in India, or at least Brooklyn Heights.

Things moved pretty quickly after that. Chris purchased state-of-the-art maritime gear (two limes and a hat). He stocked up on supplies (rum). He outfitted a first-aid kit (more rum). In a move eerily similar to current Pentagon spending, Chris bought not one boat, but three. These are the now-famous trio of ships we all know and love: the el Nino, the Pentangle, and the Santa Clara (patron saint of Aunt Bee's friends).

Captain Colon and crew spent the next five or six staggering dull weeks sailing the Atlantic, with no in-flight entertainment whatsoever other than one beat-up BetaMax copy of "H.M.S. Pinafore" and a very nervous fiddler nicknamed Teencie.

And finally, after many adventures and a mini-series starring Ed Asner, Teencie spotted land on 12 October 1492, the same year that West Virginia Senator Robert Byrd was born. After such an arduous voyage, the three crews collectively said "Yay" in Italian, and Chris named the island San Salvador, which confused the locals, who had always thought their place was called Guanahani. A petition was immediately filed for a zoning variance.

Of course, as we now know, Christopher Columbus "discovered" America in much the same way as Al Gore "invented" the internet. Lots of people were already here, running around respecting their environment and calling corn "maize." But even *those* people originally came from somewhere else, having walked across the Bering Strait as part of a time-share discount weekend giveaway. Once here, they went forth and multiplied, mostly around freeway exits, due to their new-found fondness for Stuckey's pecan logs.

Ultimately, our country was named after a different Italian explorer, a Florentine adventurer named United States Vespucci. But we still celebrate Columbus Day, because Vespucci Day rated poorly in the focus groups during the Great Marketing Synod of 1812, and Colon Day was already taken.

Columbus Day is an increasingly controversial holiday, because historians point out that millions of North America's original pecan log fans died as a direct result of contact with European peoples. And if you've ever been trapped in a poorly-ventilated United Nations elevator, you'll tend to agree.

(It's true that many humans died after Columbus landed. However, to be fair, many humans died before Columbus landed, too. But that's George Bush's fault.)

According to our internet research, Columbus Day is also known as the unofficial start of the Christmas shopping season. Personally, we take issue with that claim, because where we live, the Christmas shopping season kicks in each year around the fifth of July. We do manage to postpone decorating the downtown area until Halloween or so. But as we postpone, we pout.

We've actually seen some cities that will just leave the powered-down Christmas lights in situ, forlornly hanging up there all year long. These are usually burgs with the population of an Appalachian high school, the budget of that school's band department, and a name like Fred Unincorporated or Curdled Mohawk, Arkansas.

And don't think that Columbus Day can escape good ol' rugged American regionalism. This troubled holiday is celebrated very differently - if it's celebrated at all - depending on where in the country you happen to be.

America's first Columbus Day celebration took place in San Francisco in 1869. Among other events, there was an impromptu parade, featuring an Embarcadero exotic dancer named Lately Gaga (one of Teencie's direct descendants) and several locals costumed, more or less, as sailors. Senator Robert Byrd served as Grand Marshall.

Despite their claim to first-ever status, however, Columbus Day is not officially recognized in California. Alternatively, some California cities celebrate Indigenous People's Day, but nobody can spell "indigenous," so they just stand around comparing divorce attorneys and eating pecan logs.

The first state-wide celebration of Columbus Day was held in 1907. For some reason, it was held in Colorado, possibly due to Colorado's proximity to Santo Domingo and Cuba.

Minnesota recognizes Columbus Day, but they're not thrilled about it. Minnesotans know that America was actually discovered by the legendary Viking, Norm Van Brocklin.

Hawaii (literal translation: "The land that consonants forgot") gets in on the Columbus Day action, too, although Hawaii's not even in the same ocean. However, in Hawaii, they don't call it Columbus Day. In the Aloha State (literal translation: "Welcome! Get out!"), Columbus Day is known as "Landing Day" or, as the

155

locals say, "Aaneeuuiaamumu." (literal translation: "Continental breakfast not included")

(*According to an unconfirmed article on the internet, Columbus Day is not celebrated in South Dakota. But neither resident could be reached for comment.*)

Finally, we note that Latino communities all across America also celebrate the anniversary of Chris' first New World visit. But they call it "Dia de la Raza" (Day of the Race), and here at Internet Research Central, we have absolutely no idea what "Day of the Race" has to do with a jilted fifteenth-century Italian kid, with an agonized intestine, whose family was named after a punctuation mark.

And so it goes.

Goodbye, Columbus.

Chez Oog's Raw Bar

(A history lesson, including the first ever "Here, smell this.")

Let me ask you something. At dinner parties, have you ever been offered any food that can also, for medicinal purposes, be shoved in a mule's nose? I mean, lately?

It amazes me how we humans, throughout history, have managed to come up with some of the things we eat. How did we discover that some admittedly unlikely, often bizarre items were edible? And at what cost? How many sacrificial Europeans did we burn through while they figured out which mushrooms could be safely eaten, which mushrooms were fatal widow-makers, which mushrooms could be sold to American tourists at outrageous prices, and which mushrooms, in 1968, would cause Joe Cocker's lyrics to make sense?

Here's another example to ponder. Long ago, somewhere, some carefree (but extremely hungry) proto-human was proto-prancing around in the surf. Suddenly, he gashed himself on a cluster of rough black rocks, and immediately had two thoughts:

1) Hey, I wonder if there's anything inside that rock that I can eat?

2) Ow!

It gets better. Later that proto-afternoon, this same bruised but determined human (his name, by the way, was Oog) took a hammer to one of the black rocks, as soon as somebody invented the hammer. Inside the rock was some runny, oily thing that looked like an early outtake from "Alien." Still famished but a bit hesitant, Oog stared at the shimmering blob for a while, wondering what to call it, until his wife, Oyster, invented cocktail sauce.

And mollusks are but one example of stuff that was just lying around, stuff that we somehow decided we ought to eat. Another example is corn (or as the indigenous Americans called it, "ethanol"). Obviously, somebody once saw those tall stalks, saw those thick, fibery bulges, looked closer and thought, "Man, that is one seriously nasty worm. Wonder what's under it? Can we eat it? Did anybody invent butter yet?"

Other things aren't food, automatically. They have to become foods; in other words, they require preparation, sometimes for days and days. Pickles. Have you ever seen a recipe for homemade pickles? You have to really, really *want* to make pickles - especially if you're a disciple of the "barrel ferment" school of pickle-making, which requires an investment of 3-6 weeks, which means the recipe lasted longer than Kim Kardashian's marriage.

To be sure, there *are* people who really, really want to make pickles. One company wanted to make pickles so badly that it eschewed any concept of a marketing tie-in and just signed the first mascot that showed up for auditions: an animated stork with a Groucho Mark accent (see "mushrooms, circa 1968").

And you can't just run out and grow pickles. You have to grow cucumbers. That means somebody once saw a cucumber and thought, "You know, if I took charge of that thing for about a month, it would ROCK a cheeseburger. Did anybody invent cheese yet?"

Of course, you can't have a cheeseburger with a bun (it's in the US Constitution). How did mankind ever figure out how to make bread? Who walked through a wheat field and thought, "I'm gonna invent the sandwich! Or maybe artisan beer. Hey, who's that sad, armored guy in my wheat field? Is that Russell Crowe?"

(By the way - when somebody *did* finally invent sliced bread, how did anybody compliment them? "Great idea, Atlanta Panera! Sliced bread...why, that's the greatest thing since sli...um...uh...that's, um...")

Making dough can be complicated, unless you're the US Treasury. Some bread recipes call for sunlight, some require darkness. Some breads need to rise, some don't. (Some pushy, big-headed breads want to rise more than once, as if they thought they were Cher's career.) Some breads want yeast, some breads don't. (Yeast is a biological agent known as an "activator," a group which includes baker's yeast, natural leaven, and Al Sharpton.)

But for pure "pardon me?" value, you can't beat garum.

Single guys: Here's a handy "social graces" quiz. You're at dinner with your neighbors who, thanks to lax mortgage regulations, are second century Romans. Your host, Sirius Girth, proudly uncorks a clay jar and extends it to you, inviting you to admire its aroma. You take a quick whiff of something so foul it makes your grandparents sterile.

Select your optimal response:
a) "Mmm. Let me guess. Week-old isotope-blasted pork. North slope?"
b) "Ah! Mule medicine!"
c) "Is that smell normal, or did your aqueduct back up?"

What is this rancid liquid with the scalp-blistering smell? Meet garum.

In ancient Rome, garum was a type of fermented fish sauce. It was both a delicacy and a staple, an essential flavor in ancient Roman cooking, and one of the main reasons the ancient Romans kept running off to places like Gaul, and England, and Brooklyn.

But what *is* garum? Well, according to the internet, garum is similar to liquamen. Oh, gee, thanks. I don't know about you, but "similar to liquamen" tells me absolutely nothing. Liquamen sounds like a catchy brand name for some product made especially for single guys who can't follow those complicated instructions on tap water.

Although garum was wildly popular in the ancient Roman world, it originally came from Greece, along with other world-molding things, like the Olympics, and suffocating debt. "Garon" was the Greek name for the fish whose intestines were originally used to make garum.

That's right. Fish guts. Garum is fish guts. We took our "western civilization" cues from a clutch of ancient whack jobs who ate fish guts.

Oh, it gets better.

Not just any old fish guts. Fish guts, softened by soaking in salt, and then left out in direct sunlight for two or three months.

Somebody thought that up. Holius mackeralus. Somebody thought to do that to a fish, and then eat it. Who, for Peteus sakeus? Maybe one of those 27,000 fun-loving hearth gods. Maybe Oedipus' mom, which would explain some other things, too.

Apparently, garum was a real treat in ancient Rome, a cultural high point, which should serve as a warning to any country that's considering letting everybody run around dressed like pledges at an "Animal House" frat party. And it was economical, too - garum would keep for years, due to its high salt content, and due to the fact that nobody was exactly eager to eat something that smelled like Sunday morning behind Ulysses S. Grant's molars.

Sun-baked, three-month-old, fermented fish guts, as food. Kinda makes "Hot Pockets" look like an evening with Wolfgang Puck.

It gets better.

According to Pliny (literal translation: "of or having pline"), the ubiquitous (literal translation: "vile molar breath") garum also had medicinal values, for humans *and* animals. For example, it was used to treat bone spavin in horses and mules, and was said to cure scabies in sheep.

(NOTE FROM OUR STAFF: For the half-dozen or so of you out there who aren't 2,000-year-old ancient Roman veterinarians: Bone spavin is not a disease - it's actually a theatrical device, wherein ancient Roman vets would artificially pad their bills by following these simple steps: remove the scholarly glasses, pinch the bridge of the nose, sigh defeatedly, and then interject vague terms like 'hock joint,' 'tarsometatarsal articulation' and 'Royal Lipizzaner submission fee.')

(NOTE FROM OUR STAFF: Scabies, by the way, is a contagious skin disease marked by excessive scratching, and you haven't really lived a rich, full life till you've seen a sheep trying to scratch its own back.)

(NOTE FROM OUR STAFF: We should note that 'Bone Spavin' would be a great name for a band.)

Garum was considered a good antidote for dog bites, and crocodile bites, too, as long as your HMO plan covered giant lizard wounds *and* brutally skank-smelling generics.

Other ancient Roman healers, especially those with excellent malpractice insurance, used garum as a treatment for everything from ulcers to dysentery, from sciatica to sea dragon bites (for more on sea dragons, see "mushrooms, circa 1968"). Garum was often prescribed as a laxative and, given what garum is made of, that's probably redundant.

Garum was also used to treat animals. And here, our story leaps past "strange" and rushes straight to "downright odd." As the late Hunter S. Thompson might say, "When the going gets weird, the weird turn pro."

Imagine you're an ancient Roman horse with phlegm issues. (That exact phrase, by the way, was part of the proposal that led directly to the Kim Kardashian wedding. Or divorce.) Then suddenly one morning, your owner, Bifidus Regularis, reads an article about horse and mule phlegm (it was a slow news day) on the front stone of *The Daily Stele* ("All the news that's fit to chisel"), a piece penned by those two famous veterinarians, Vegetius (literal translation: "meat & three") and Pelagonius (literal translation: "Sid Caesar"). And then, heeding the advice of experts, your owner decides to treat your problem by pouring a gallon of garum in your nose.

How humiliating! And what can you do? Who do you get in touch with? It's not like you can retire to a stud farm, because nobody's invented Kentucky yet.

And it's not an option for the likes of you, an aging equus, to make a scene - to just snort, cavil and complain.

After all, down the via a piece, somebody just invented glue.

Politics: First-Degree Felony Stupid

~*~*~

"The reason there are so few female politicians is that it is too much trouble to put makeup on two faces."

Maureen Murphy

~*~*~*~*~

Man of the Peephole

(Oh, what a tangled world wide web we weave)

You know, if you're a writer who writes about dumb stuff in current events, what a rich, odd summer it's been! Case in point: normally, if one had a plan to pen something about politicians, one would eventually have to mention politics. Normally.

Not lately.

And if you want dumb, you can always depend on American politicians to deliver. Everyone remembers that memorable bromide, "All politics is, or are, local, or stupid," ascribed to former Speaker of the House Tip O'Neill, although he personally attributed the phrase to his father, Tatum.

But this summer, it seems someone's ratcheted up Dumb in D.C. As Hunter Thompson might have put it, "when the going gets weird, the weird turn pro."

Granted, there *are* political tales to be told, to be sure. After all, we're facing the 2012 election season, which officially began at 7:01 PM on 4 November 2008. In fact, the rule-free vote-fest that we call the "American political system" shares a unique honor with the Great Wall of China - these are the only two manmade objects on Earth that can be seen from outer space, if you don't count Geraldo Rivera's moustache.

So there's no shortage of political targets. For example, former Alaskan Governor (and quadrennial potential Presidential candidate) Sarah Palin made headlines when she announced a bus tour.

Personally, it takes me almost no time at all to tour a bus.

Just a few days ago, thousands of Alaskan emails from Governor Palin's term were thawed, printed, crated up, and delivered to the public. No, I *don't* know why. Avid Alaskan email analysts who, sadly, have no life of their own, eagerly dived into the collection, and NBC's Brian Williams plans to personally interview several of the emails.

And have no doubt - the analysts will find *something* to Eureka about in that email tonnage. They'll turn up something, like, oh, Mama Grizzly once complaining about an under-toasted bagel, which clearly proves she is an anti-Zionist, or pro-Pop Tart.

In a related story, the election season's moron marathon witnessed an unprecedented political disaster from the Republican bench, when everyone on the "Newt Gingrich for

President" staff did not abandon ship; however, Newt himself resigned.

In global news, the International Monetary Fund was hacked by an eight-year-old using his smart phone and a modified banking app. When it was all said and done, billionaire George Soros found that his entire fortune had been donated to a conservative-leaning Baskin-Robbins in Dayton, Ohio.

Oddly enough, our Defense Department admitted to a similar security breach, as the Pentagon's procurement system was hacked by a rogue calculator virus. As it turns out, the virus reviewed some of the military's math, got embarrassed and, unable to stop itself, made a few recalculations, resulting in a savings of several billion dollars.

Meanwhile, a raging wildfire in Arizona jumped the state line, crossing into New Mexico. That action brought the blaze into the realm of the bloated Interstate Commerce clause (which is also visible from outer space), so Congress immediately taxed combustion. New Mexico petitioned the Fed for assistance, and a few billion in mortgage adjustments, a move championed by several terra cotta potters at a liberal-leaning equine therapy seminar in Taos. Due to a miscommunication, FEMA rushed emergency supplies to Santa Claus and Tina Fey, and Homeland Security issued an Ember Alert.

Of course, the story that's grasped everyone by the ... ah ... the, um ... the ... the story that's got everyone talking is our hesitant peek into the bawdy antics of a certain lewd member of the House of Representatives.

The story unfolded almost as quickly as the lies unraveled. After days of total denial and outright outrage, the apparently self-appointed leader of the "Raucous Caucus" found himself guilty of full frontal stupidity.

Yes, him. The one with the funny name. That bizarre buff-monster, that Twitter twit, that self-serving self-photographer, that ego zeppelin, that monument to hubris: Congressman Ballpark Frank.

Sure, his name didn't help matters. I mean, when you're named after something that men buy from other men at sporting events, you're bound to have a few stability issues here and there.

But then, like the Arizona wildfire, the silliness spread. Whenever anyone heard the news, and the names *in* the news, they started to snicker. And suddenly, everything became a double entendre. Everything. It was insane. A typical conversation at the office water cooler:

"I would like to have some cabbage slaw for lunch."
"Yeah, I just bet you would."

And from there, it quickly got out of control. People gasping, blushing, complaining to Human Resources.

Like many self-inflicted episodes in life, it was simultaneously sad and funny. A mirror-kissing moron in Congress who thinks he's attractive enough to take very un-Alaskan photos of himself, and then sends them to a child that's young enough to be his parole officer's daughter, using an unsecured social network where the chief literary attraction is a fictional farm.

What next, Ballpark? Circus animals? Interns with pizzas?

The jokes flew. "Is that a Congressman in your pocket, or are you just glad to see m ... never mind. What was I thinking? Of *course* there's a Congressman in your pocket."

And he just kept digging a deeper hole for his dumb self. It was like watching a politically-pointed remake of Oscar Wilde's classic tale, "The Picture of Dorian Gray," as Ballpark Frank's career faded, and faded, and faded:

"Absolutely, I didn't do it!"
"I was hacked!"
"I didn't do it."
"I think I was hacked."
"I don't think I did it."
"You can't prove I did it."
"I got people looking into it to see if I did it."
"Maybe I did it."
"Okay, I did it, but I didn't break any laws while I did it."
"Okay, she looked sixteen to me."
"...re-elect me?"
"...please?"
"...plea..."
"...pl..."

Soon, his own political cronies stopped returning his calls. One party leader, a lady from Florida, made it very clear that he should resign. I forget the lady's name but, based on her haircut, I think it was Congresswoman Labradoodle.

But no. He wouldn't go. Ballpark Frank was made of sterner stuff. A man who can stand unsheathed in front of a taxpayer-funded gymnasium mirror and go all Olan Mills at himself is not gonna just hop the next Greyhound.

No. Like any politician worth having a vote to purchase, the Congressbiped capitalized.

First, we heard that he was allegedly photographed wearing a promotional box of Fruity Pebbles. Ballpark claimed that somebody had hacked his online grocery account and had then sent a bogus Harris Teeter. A spokesman said that someone was looking into Ballpark's box.

Next, we learned that he might resign after all and expatriate to Europe, where he planned to accept a lucrative offer, performing suggestive interpretive dance routines during Bunga Bunga parties at the estate of Italian Prime Minister Sylvio Berlusconi.

Lastly, rumors were floated that Ballpark was being courted by clothing giant, The Men's Under-Wearhouse, to pen an endorsement deal promoting a new slogan: "You're gonna like the way I look, if you can prove that's the way I look."

And, in the end, karma kicked in. In a classic case of poetic justice, the occasionally stark Congressflasher, Ballpark Frank, was molested by his own ego.

Think about it. These days, we have email and instant messaging. We have chat, texting, cell phones, cell phones with cameras, Facebook, Twitter. These days, privacy eludes.

Imagine what a vile, sordid, Sodomitic cesspool Washington D.C. must have been, back in the days *before* they got caught...

As Lily Tomlin might have put it: "We're the Government. We don't care. We don't have to."

Full Frontal Stupidity

What's the Plural of Y'all?

(The Second Oldest Profession meets the Bible Belt)

It's the middle of January, 2012, the Republican Presidential hopefuls have descended upon my state, South Carolina, and it is an absolute nuthouse down here. I don't see any way to escape the madness, except one: maybe the Mayans miscalculated.

Maybe, just maybe, the Mayans misread their round rock clock, and the world will end early. I don't see any other way to avoid this ongoing political ego parade.

But Mayans or not, I think we can say this with some certainty: the world probably will end wa-a-ay before this endless election season does.

But for now, it's South Carolina's job to help pick the President. And the contestants? They're all here:

- Willard Mitt 'Glove' Romney (he squeaked a win in Iowa by ... what? ... seven votes? Basically, he won Iowa by a family)
- Brick Sanitarium and his sweater-vest collection (who looks like an under-aged son from an Iowan family)
- Nude King Grinch (whose ego is the size of an Iowan family)
- Tron Paul (he fights for the users)
- Rick Prairie (I'm pretty sure he's not an actual human, but an animated cartoon character from 'Toy Story')
- Jon Huntsman's son, John Huntsman, who is Jon Huntsman's son

Just making it out of Iowa alive must've been tough. I remember hearing an Iowa politician make this biologically complex promise: "When my head and my heart come together I'll jump in with both feet."

Whoa. Never change metaphors in the middle of streaming the rules for a game horse's level playing field.

While in Iowa, Rick Prairie, in between power-grinning, eating fried lard on a stick, and power-grinning, described Iowans as "just hard-workin' God-fearin' freedom-lovin' people." So please consider making a donation to the Rick Prairie campaign, so they can afford to buy a box of lower-case Gs.

And remember - after Iowa, Herman Cain suspended his Presidential campaign. And he's STILL polling at 8%. At this rate, if he drops out entirely, he'll win.

But after leaving Iowa (their favorite state) and New Hampshire (their favorite state) all six surviving candidates have now invaded South Carolina (their favorite state). And they're everywhere - in the parks, on the news, in the diners and on the phones.

As you'd imagine, it's getting ugly, too. Just today, Nude King Grinch accused Willard Romney of speaking French in public. Tron Paul immediately demanded that we withdraw our troops from Willard Romney. Willard could not be reached for comment, since he was campaigning in the South Carolina Upstate, while his hair was holding a rally on the coast.

To be sure, you other forty-nine States should be a bit concerned that South Carolina is playing such a pivotal role in your destiny. Keep in mind that South Carolina is a place where one food group is pork barbecue, and beef barbecue is the other one. (Barbecue *sauce*, on the other hand, is not a food group. Barbecue sauce, if it's done right, is a divine appointment from heaven.)

We have our own language, too. We pronounce Manigault as 'mannigoe' and Simons as 'simmons.' We pronounce boyfriend as 'beau' but Beaufort as 'byoofurt.' And we still pronounce carpetbagger as 'collateral damage.'

In South Carolina, we know that one person is "y'all" and we know that the plural of y'all is "all y'all." We make a clear distinction between 'dinner' and 'supper' but we make no distinction at all between 'Can you believe what that clueless idiot just did?' and Aw, bless his heart.'

177

We have cities with suggestive names like Ninety Six, Six Mile and Due West. We have a town called North and a burg named Norway.

Not long ago, in Norway (population: dwindling), the outgoing Mayor refused to give the City Hall keys to the incoming Mayor. So the incoming Mayor broke in to City Hall by breaking out, and crawling in, a window. Shortly, the outgoing Mayor of Norway had the incoming Mayor of Norway arrested, but the incoming Mayor bribed a jail guard with a pint of pork barbecue. The incoming Mayor escaped and fled to Sweden (yes, there is). From there, he hopped a NASCAR convoy to Finland (yes, there is) and ultimately was sent back to Norway after being extradited by Denmark (yes, there is).

It may surprise you to hear it, but here in South Carolina, we're regularly treated to groundbreaking research and brilliant news analysis, resulting in headlines like this one:

LAKE WATER LEVELS RISE WITH RAINFALL

Whoa. Somebody alert the National Weather Service. Somebody call the Nobel committee.

And how about this one:

"...the bust was dubbed Operation Countywide because it was conducted from one end of the county to the other."

Whoa. You know, sometimes it's hard to see the Forrest for the Gump.

Here's another:

"At a bowling alley in Rock Hill, a man was charged with attempted murder after he threw a bowling ball at a woman who rejected his offer to buy her a drink."

See, folks, *Virginia* is for lovers. South Carolina is for hunter-gatherers.

And, once upon a time, we had a Governor who confuses marital infidelity with mountain hiking, and who apparently thinks North Carolina is in Brazil.

Finally, we offer a quick pop quiz. Ready?

Outside, it's raining in bright sunshine. Here in South Carolina, this means what?
1) the devil's beating his wife
2) our former Governor is 'hiking' with the devil's wife
3) an angel just got its wings, and then sold them at the flea market
4) you're about to witness relative humidity that actually climbs *ABOVE* 100%

Starting to get the picture? This is why somebody once described South Carolina as "too small to be a country, too big to be an insane asylum."

And speaking of asylums, here's a quick Politico Update: Brick Sanitarium has taken a commanding lead in South Carolina, after switching from sleeveless sweater-vests to sleeveless plaid work shirts.

Another update: we've just learned that South Carolina's Governor has endorsed Willard. This is our current Governor, mind you, not the one with the backpack full of travel visas, tacos and tequila.

By the way - North, South Carolina? It's south of the South Carolina state capital.

And North, South Carolina is 100 miles southeast of Due West.

Return of the Giant Vote-Sucking Locusts

(The good news: it's only every four years. The bad news: it lasts for five.)

Moderator: Good evening, America! Welcome to the Iowa State Fair and the first of several hundred thousand election events!

(Cue applause prompt)

Moderator: I'm your rugged-yet-sensitive host, Biff Condor, reminding you that, here at Wolf News, we're State Fair and Balanced!

(Cue audio of insanely expensive "24x7 political coverage" jingle)

Moderator: We're glad you're with us tonight! On behalf of Wolf News, thanks to our studio audience here at the Iowa State Fair, and to our viewers tuning in from home, many of whom still have jobs.

(Cue fear-inspiring "breaking news" graphic of national debt clock)

Moderator: Before we get started, let me tell you a little more about myself. I'm Biff Condor, award-winning, all-purpose Hair Helmet and international camera magnet. I'm a regular recipient of TV's prestigious Em-Me award, an honor recognizing my uncanny ability to inject myself into absolutely any news story whatsoever, regardless of whether or not I was actually there. But enough about me, the award-winning telejournalist, Biff Condor. Now, without further ado, let's cut to several minutes of car commercials, featuring apocalyptic price deadlines, screaming off-camera announcers and squinting local businessmen dressed in bad suits.

(Cue commercial)

Moderator: Welcome back to our coverage of tonight's event, including various camera shots of my head. I'm award-winning broadcast legend, Biff Condor. And now, without further ado, let's cut to several minutes of real estate commercials, featuring great discounts on desolate, bone-arid, pre-electricity, Obama-forsaken ranch properties in Vulture Jerky, Idaho and Barren Tonsil, Wyoming.

(Cue commercial)

Moderator: Welcome back! I'm your air-brushed host, Biff Condor. And now, without further ado, let's introduce the 2012 Republican candidates for President, each of whom has spent the previous week uttering mystical pronouncements that always begin with '*at the end of the day*' or '*where the rubber meets the road.*' All week long, we've watched them smiling while flipping hamburgers, or smiling while autographing hamburgers, or pointing and acting surprised when they see someone semi-famous who was planted in the audience. America, please give a warm welcome to Glove Romney, Michele "Toots" Bachwommann, Tim "Toots" Aplenty, Guido "I'm Not John McCain" Cain, Eft "Newt" Gingrich, Sanctum Santorum, and Thaddeus Somebody.

(Cue applause prompt)

Ron St. Paul: And me! And me!

Moderator: Oh, yeah.

(Cue montage reel of Biff Condor's career)

Moderator: Tonight, we'll be asking our candidates very probing questions, composed and hand-written in a lovely award-winning cursive by me, Biff Condor. We'll begin with Glove Romney, who's been running for President non-stop since about 1928 and who is the only candidate named after a baseball appliance. I should point out that I, your humble correspondent, Biff Condor, used to play baseball. Good evening, Glove.

Romney: Hi, Biff. I'm accompanied tonight by my wife Wheel Play, my sons Bunt, Bullpen and Ground Rule Double, and my hair, which just formed its own garage band. I'd like to say thanks to the people of Iowa for watching me simultaneously smile and flip hamburgers, and that's why, when the rubber meets the road, I'm clearly the most qualified person on this platform.

Moderator: And now, let's turn to Guido Cain. Guido, as the only "person of color" on this stage or, for that matter, in the entire state of Iowa, let's start with the most relevant question that I, Biff Condor, can compose; one that pierces through the "politically correct" veneer and addresses this crucial element of America's troubled past and promising future: Thin crust or deep dish?

Cain: When I was the godfather at Big Caesar's Pizza King, I made business decisions every day, at the end of the day. I know how to focus on the problem and fix it in 30 minutes or less. Guaranteed. And that's what the American people are clamoring for.

Moderator: Thank you, Guido. Well, having touched on pizza, that wraps up our segment on America's foreign policy, and I think you'll agree that our in-depth treatment of America's foreign policy is at *least* as competent as anything going on in the current administration. So now, let's pivot like a laser...

(*rim shot*)

Moderator: ...to a discussion of domestic issues. But first, let's cut to several minutes of commercials in which you'll be repeatedly yelled at by a bald, angry Watergate ex-con about why you should invest in gold.

(*Cue commercial*)

184

Moderator: Welcome back. I'm award-winning media icon, Biff Condor. Before we move on to our next candidate, let's take a minute to review tonight's rules and procedures. Each candidate will have exactly one minute to speak, and if anybody on tonight's stage actually *complies* with that rule, nobody will be more surprised than me. This one-minute rule may be the most ignored instruction in the history of mankind, with the possible exception of those cautions about not removing that tag from your mattress. Anyway, each candidate will ha...

Sanctum Santorum: Excuse me, Biff, but is anybody gonna talk to me tonight?

Moderator: I seriously doubt it.

Santorum: But my experien...

Moderator: As I was saying, each candidate will have thirty seconds for rebuttal, which is an ancient French term meaning "snide, bitter and staggeringly irrelevant comment." Also, throughout tonight's debate, candidates will have ample opportunity to be captured on camera rolling their eyes, furiously scribbling notes, or shaking their heads in poignant "tragic hero" gestures of silent disgust.

Santorum: But they told me if I smiled and flipped hambur...

Moderator: Zip it, Richie Cunningham. Now, concerning tonight's procedures, I should warn the studio audience that, from time to time, you may hear short bursts from an alarm bell.

185

That has nothing to do with our debate, or violations of the one-minute rule, or anything like that. It's just that ... uh ... it's, um ... well, let's put it this way. Remember - outside, at the State Fair, there are thousands of professionally obese rural people swilling cheap beer, gobbling barrel-loads of undercooked pork, and sampling all manner of ill-prepared fried things that have been mutating for hours under a broiling mid-summer sun. For those of you unfamiliar with rural customs in the "flyover" States, this confluence can create a sudden meteorological condition known as an "orographic flatulence pendant echo" - or as locals put it - St. Elmo's Fire Drill.

(Cue 'Wizard of Oz' tornado scene)

Moderator: Well, there it is. That's who we are and how we ride. Out here in Fried Lard country, cyclones ain't the only things that kill, and storm cellars ain't the only things that save. And speaking of Iowa, let's turn now to our next candidate, Michele Bachwommann.

Bachwommann: Good evening, Biff. It's great to be back home in Iowa where, at the end of the day every summer, I used to flip burgers while smiling and eat fried lard on a stick. This went on until I got so desperately sick of Iowa that even a place like Minnesota began to look good. And that's why I'm the only candidate on this stage who will fix America's energy dependency on foreign immigration corn tariffs while balancing the serious shortage of education-ready shovels.

Eft "Newt" Gingrich: Biff, may I offer a rebuttal?

Moderator: Well, technically, no, since nobody asked your opinion in the first place.

Gingrich: But I'm practically a Statesman. I have white hair!

Moderator: And you're named after a salamander.

Gingrich: Look, when the rubber hits the end of the day, I'm the only candi...

Moderator: And now to ... um ... Thaddeus Whaddayacallit. Senator, or whatever you did, any comments, or any update on your attempt at generating a visible emotion or a recognizable facial expression?

Thad: First, let me respo...

Moderator: Thank you, sir, but you're out of time. "Toots" Aplenty, if you'll please stand up, you can respond.

Aplenty: I *am* standing up.

Moderator: Awkward. And finally, let's turn to an absent Governor of Texas who only became an official candidate about eleven minutes ago and, surprisingly, is already leading in the polls. Governor, would you like to add anything before I, Biff Condor, award-winning Thesaurus owner and author of the upcoming book, "Biff On Biff," wrap things up?

Disembodied voice of a Texas Governor: I am the only candidate on this stage who is not on this stage. Vote for me, or I'll kill your cow.

Moderator: Be sure to stay tuned for my weekly news round-up, "Running Hunched Over Across Various Wind-Whipped Landscapes with Biff Condor." And thanks again to our candidates for showing up tonight, despite the fact that most of them have about as much chance of becoming President as fried lard on a stick.

Ron St. Paul: And me! And me!

Moderator: Oh, yeah.

How Will Ya Spin It?

(fib ipsa loquitor -- the lie speaks for itself)

[cue theme music]

Good evening, ladies and gentlemen, and welcome to an all-new episode of "How Will Ya Spin It?" ... the game show where political hopefuls prepare for a profitable career in self-serving public service! I'm your host, Robin Taxim.

[cue applause]

And now, I'd like to introduce tonight's three politicians! I'd *like to*, but I can't, because *they're not here!*

[rim shot]

Unfortunately, contestant Number One couldn't be here tonight, because he's busy showing up unexpectedly at the Iowa State Fair, which is a pure coincidence that has nothing to do with the upcoming election season.

Contestant Number Two is not here, either, because she's busy showing up unexpectedly in her favorite state, New Hampshire, which has suddenly replaced Iowa as her favorite state until tomorrow, when she travels to her favorite state, South Carolina, on her way to her favorite state, Florida.

And contestant Number Three was unable to make it tonight, because he's planning to make an announcement shortly about an announcement to announce his plans to form an exploratory group tasked with gauging public opinion about his plans to announce his formation of an political action committee. However, he did swing by and vote "Present" so we would validate his parking, and he would like to remind our studio audience that was for showing up before he was against it.

[cue theme music]

Not to worry! During the ten years we've been on the air here at "How Will Ya Spin It?" politicians have promised to show up every single week, and we haven't seen one yet!

[rim shot]

Anyway, all of you already know how we play "How Will Ya Spin It?" We confront you viewers at home with a dozen ethical or political challenges, and it's up to you to pick the best way to spin it! So let's get started, eh?

[cue applause]

Okay, Challenge Number One: You're an average, run-of-the-mill politician; in other words, you're under indictment and you cheat on your spouse. Your major re-election donors insist you support legislation to deregulate pharmaceutical research, but your staff discovers that the new drug would cause anyone with a larynx to turn yellow and explode.

Audience?

[audience] HOW WILL YA SPIN IT?

---------- | | ----------

A: Vote "Present."

B: Blame George Bush.

C: Hold a barbecue to raise money for the victims of UDE ("Unplanned Dermal Expansion").

---------- | | ----------

Challenge Two: You've wrapped up another grueling three-day work week, a week that included several luncheons and cheating on your spouse. You decide to spend the rest of the month on a taxpayer-funded "fact-finding" jaunt to Aruba, but you're challenged by a citizen watchdog group.

How will ya spin it?

---------- | | ----------

A: Arrange an exclusive interview with the hosts of "Aruban Idol."

B: Cancel the trip and hide out in a hotel with the Wisconsin legislature.

C: Point to internet chatter about al Qaeda targeting reggae music.

---------- | | ----------

Challenge: Your "holier than thou" ethical crusader image has gone a bit inky, due to some minor moral inconsistencies, like getting hundred-dollar haircuts, fathering an out-of-wedlock child, and robbing donors of several hundred thousand dollars (which you stole to help cover up cheating on your spouse).
How will ya spin it?

---------- | | ----------

A: Blame the right-wing media for conspiratorial witch-hunting.

B: Post social media videos of you cutting your own hair.

C: Schedule a press conference. Let people know that you feel so ashamed, you can barely enjoy your "global warming" conference in Aruba. During the presser, be sure you're not holding a Mai Tai.

---------- | | ----------

Challenge: You're a fairly normal (albeit astonishingly dull) career politician. But one day, perhaps due to some severe childhood head injury, you have a psychotic episode of historic proportions, during which you make the staggeringly insane claim that you invented the Internet.
How will ya spin it?

---------- | | ----------

A: Ghost-write a book titled "An Inconvenient Untruth."

B: Blame George Bush.

C: Donate your larynx to a victim of UDE. After all, *you're* not using it.

---------- | | ----------

Challenge: You somehow get tricked into holding a Town Hall meeting, during which you have to actually talk to those faceless drones from back home who keep re-electing you. During an impassioned question from one of your constituents, your cell phone rings. You notice that it's your broker, getting back to you with an illegal insider-trading tip.

How will ya spin it?

---------- | | ----------

A: Take the call. Voters are idiots, and will forget all about it by November.

B: Take the call. Find out where the constituent lives and name a Post Office after her.

C: Take the call. Leak that the constituent may be cheating on her spouse. Then raise taxes.

---------- | | ----------

Challenge: In order to get re-elected, you promised the Rotarians a new nuclear power plant. You promised the Moose Club a downwind coal-fired battery array. You promised PETA a peat-powered windmill farm, and you promised the Quakers an Ordnung-friendly power grid fueled solely by kinetic energy generating from rubbing two Amish Boy Scouts together. Meanwhile, you secretly accepted 113 taozillion dollars from a Chinese company to back legislation legalizing off-shore generators that produce electricity from diced yak parts.

How will ya spin it?

---------- | | ----------

A: Deny you ever met with the Chinese government.

B: Deny you ever ate Chinese food.

C: Learn Mandarin.

---------- | | ----------

Challenge: A picture surfaces on the Internet, and some charge that it's a "candid" shot of you in your underwear and that you, a married man, facebooked the photo to a coed intern who is underage, and is on a terrorist watch list, and is an illegal alien, and who used to date your spouse. To complicate matters, the underwear's made of leather. With reinforced grommets that spell out your initials. Plus, it's a plus-sized ladies' corset.

How will ya spin it?

---------- | | ----------

A: Claim you have no idea who's in the underwear, but you have people looking into it.

B: Claim your social media account was hacked. By George Bush.

C: Raise taxes on leather imports.

---------- | | ----------

Challenge: In order to get re-elected, you promised your constituents that they would be taller if they would just vote for you. Obviously, you were lying, a habit you embrace with a furious intensity, as if lying were seven of the Ten Commandments. Nobody got any taller, of course, with the exception of that one family who lives out by the Rotary Club's nuclear power plant.

How will ya spin it?

---------- | | ----------

A: Lower knee-caps in the other forty-nine States.

B: Blame George Bush.

C: Outlaw height.

---------- | | ----------

Challenge: You'd like to run for President, even though you grew up in another country, and you've never had a private sector job outside of academia, and your two-sentence resume consists of organizing "Save Our Swing-Set" neighborhood fundraisers, and you can't articulate a coherent sentence without reading from a teleprompter. You'd like to cheat on your spouse, but the last time you made her angry, she hit you with the teleprompter. During the campaign, an obviously biased reporter dares to question your credentials.

How will ya spin it?

---------- | | ----------

A: You invite the reporter on a Lake Michigan fishing weekender with a guy named Tony the Fixer.

B: You obfuscate by demanding to see Donald Trump's birth certificate.

C: You point out that you did, after all, draw that sword from the stone.

---------- | | ----------

Challenge: You'd like to run for President again, based on your long-standing tradition of running for President, and also because you have some kind of weird, wind-proof hair-helmet with follicles that haven't moved since Gutenberg invented the analog Kindle. Pundits posit that your coif could cope with an EF-4 tornado. Plus, you're named after a baseball glove.

How will ya spin it?

---------- | | ----------

A: Wear starched white dress shirts, every day, until voters are numbed into thinking all the other candidates are just bohemian flannel-tramps.

B: Cash in that "One Hundred Times Is The Charm" teeth-capping coupon.

C: Point out that your religion once supported polygamy, which kind of makes cheating on your spouse redundant, if not downright masochistic.

---------- | | ----------

Challenge: You've been indicted for misappropriation of campaign funds, cheating on your spouse, tax fraud, lying under oath and dating a farm animal.

How will ya spin it?

---------- | | ----------

A: Go on record as being firmly pro-Farm Subsidy.

B: Blame Old MacDonald.

C: Counter with the argument, "Well, I may have my faults, but at least I'm not a heterosexual Christian."

---------- | | ----------

And tonight's final Challenge: You're the target of an FBI sting operation, during which you were filmed purchasing Aruba, charging it to your government credit card, and cheating on your spouse.

Audience?

[audience] HOW WILL YA SPIN IT?

---------- | | ----------

A: Donate your credit card points to charity.

B: Blame George Bush.

C: Announce your re-election campaign.

---------- | | ----------

[cue applause]

Well, folks, that wraps up another episode of "How Will Ya Spin It!" My thanks to our studio audience and to those of you tuning in from home!

[cue theme music]

And remember the "How Will Ya Spin It?" motto, folks ... as a famous actor once said:

"The most important thing in this job is *sincerity*. Once you can fake *that*, you've got it made!"

[rim shot]

How To Survive Disaster Advice

(Your tax dollars at work. Well, somebody's tax dollars.)

Hi there, citizen! (or, in case we hit a needle in a haystack - Hi there, taxpayer!) Welcome to another official, expensive, and ultimately useless government publication!

OFFICIAL MISSION STATEMENT: FEMA (the "Feral Excitement Manipulation Agency") and the Bureau of Indian Affairs ("huh?") are proud to bring you this official Disaster Preparedness publication, prepared at great expense ("yours, not ours") and completely updated ("we changed the font") in painstaking detail ("we whipped it up this morning").

OFFICIAL DISCLAIMER: You may be asking yourself: What in the name of Tonto & The Three Stooges does the Bureau of Indian Affairs have to do with disaster preparedness? Well, not much. We admit that. But then, take a quick look around at recent disasters, and be honest.

Neither does FEMA.

To be honest, the Bureau of Indian Affairs hasn't been relevant since their field trip to go watch "The Last of the Mohicans." But the Bureau is part of this project for an entire different reason. What with all the recent whining about Washington's over-spending, your government's been catching a lot of flak for a lot of things, like having an entire department dedicated to the sex life of native Americans. So we do what we do best - we just dim the lights and shove that department's budget around as needed, like we do with any Federal spending that comes under scrutiny (wait till you hear about the "Grebe" initiative, and all the taxpayer money being spent to relocate socially stressed ducks).

Welcome to Civil Service!

But let's get back to our mission. Here at FEMA, we understand - life can jump up behind you. And we want to do our part to help you get ready for any life-altering eventualities, such as hurricanes, earthquakes, particularly steamy Indian affairs, or absurdly incompetence from your Federal government.

In a normal year, DHS & FEMA get to be incompetent once or twice. But 2011 was no normal year. Before the madness finally ended, the 2011 Storm Season claimed the lives of thousands and thousands of daytime television hours. Those hours, America can never replace.

Of course, there were human tragedies, too. During the nearly historic 2011 earthquake, which was almost felt in as many as one places, a Cape Cod wedding caterer was wounded in Bed Bath & Beyond when a pallet of cranberry bog-themed paper plates collapsed. Then, late in the tropical storm season (Hurricane Yahtzee), a pedestrian in Virginia was struck by an airborne used-car salesman during the last-minute filming of a "this weekend only" TV commercial. (Remember, people - during a hurricane, an un-tethered car dealer can become a life-threatening missile.)

And disasters in 2011 weren't limited to foul weather. In August, the middle of a perfectly clear day, a house-bound man in Elk Nostril, North Carolina succumbed to a heart attack after repeatedly watching Super Bowl clips of Janet Jackson's wardrobe malfunction.

And so, to prepare you for exposure to painful things like natural disasters, or civil service employees, we've put together this Disaster Preparedness quiz.

Ready? Let's begin:

Q: FEMA exists under the organizational umbrella of what overarching agency?
1. The Department of Homeland Security
2. *America's Most Wanted*
3. China

Q: The name of the current Secretary of Homeland Security is
1. Janet Neapolitan
2. Janet Reno
3. Janet Jackson

Q: What does it take for a 24x7 cable news channel to shift into non-stop emergency news mode?
1. An Atlantic storm system with sustained measurable pressure below 950 millibars
2. Sweeps Week
3. Dawn

Q: Once storm-generated winds reach 40 miles per hour, what happens?
1. 911 operators may refuse to dispatch emergency vehicles
2. Electric cars may flip over, fail to navigate hilly terrain, or just faint
3. If you're Mitt Romney's hair, absolutely nothing

Q: As a result of the almost historic 2011 Quake, hundreds of thousands of citizens along America's Eastern Seaboard
1. Nearly lost their homes and everything they owned
2. Nearly lost their interest in the almost historic 2011 Quake
3. Nearly lost their balance

Q: Once storm-generated winds reach 80 miles per hour, what happens?
1. The White House may have to call in FEMA
2. The White House may have to call up the National Guard
3. The White House may have to call out for delivery pizza

Q: The reason TV news reporters stand out on the beach in the middle of community-destroying Category 500 hurricanes is

1. They cling to an admirable, deep-seated, lifelong respect for the First Amendment
2. They are bound by an unshakeable, heroic duty to inform a grateful American public
3. It was either that, or go cover the Grand Opening of yet another Italian Ice franchise

Q: "The Last of the Mohicans" was a film about
1. An Indian named Natty Bumppo
2. An Indian named Buddy Mohican
3. Out-sourced phone support for satellite dish TV

Q: There is an American sub-culture, popularly called "Storm Trackers," who actually like to chase storms and see how close they can get without becoming dead, or maimed, or extremely flat. Such people are
1. What population-control sociologists like to call "self-pruning"
2. Not likely to attend Yanni concerts
3. Rare. Eventually.

Q: "Ten Little Indians" was a film about
1. The making of a Janet Jackson video
2. Agatha Christie's years of intensive therapy with the Bureau of Indian Affairs
3. The penultimate Mohicans

Q: When the government "highly recommends" you vacate your property immediately, you should
1. Trust them and leave immediately, given the crackerjack job they've done at handling everything else

2. Leave immediately, unless you drive an electric car with a bumper that couldn't survive a glancing blow by a jaywalking ferret

3. Make sure the evacuation order came from *our* government

Q: New York City just can't seem to get a break. After an earthquake and then a hurricane, the Big Apple will next have to face

1. Godzilla
2. A massive outbreak of United Nations parking violations
3. Another "Die Hard" remake

Q: The role of a Hurricane Hunter pilot is to

1. Measure wind velocities near the eye of a storm
2. Cull the human race of maniac daredevils who might otherwise become commercial airline pilots (see "self-pruning")
3. Try not to weep uncontrollably while your plane is being attacked like a spiral-cut ham at a "Legalize Pot" convention

Q: Once storm-generated winds reach 100 miles per hour, what happens?

1. Satellite dish TV reception may fail. But then, that can happen during wind gusts of up to 1 mile per hour.
2. Politicians in Virginia start campaigning in West Virginia
3. Homeland Security points out that very few hurricanes enter the U.S. via the Arizona border

Q: When stocking up for a pending emergency, the most important provisions to remember are
1.   Water, Batteries & First Aid Supplies
2.   Water Purification Tablets, Can Openers & Generators
3.   Lawyers, Guns & Money

Q: And speaking of disaster preparedness, Moses long ago parted the Red Sea in an attempt to escape from
1.   Egyptian daytime television
2.   Taxation without representation
3.   Janet Jackson

Well, there you have it! From all of us at FEMA and other cash-bloated agencies, like the Department of Metrosexual Mallard & Grebe Relocation, thanks for your time ... and we hope you survive lots of stuff!

And if not, enjoy your $255 government death benefit!

Southern Discomfort

(The critical role of sausage biscuits in South Carolina politics)

You might have missed it. You might have slept right through it. After all, it took place on a lazy mid-winter Saturday.

Plus, the college football season was over, having been replaced by the wildly popular sport of league bowling, where you almost never get to see any serious violence.

So you might have missed it. Maybe you were busy preparing your tailgating smorgasbord, before watching the breathtaking Professional Bowling US Open (*brought to you by Lumber Liquidators!*), featuring all your favorite Alley Warriors, who, for some unexplained reason, all have names like Mike Wzmlrzksi.

But this Saturday, here in South Carolina, *we* were getting ready to pick the next President.

Right after breakfast.

See, all this week, we've been trying our best to be polite, as the full slate of candidates careened across our state - staffers, know-it-alls, nabobs and news crews in tow - tying up traffic and babbling bromides, kissing hands and shaking babies, disrupting routine and interrupting breakfast, at diner after diner after diner.

Don't get me wrong - in South Carolina, our role in picking a President is a responsibility we take very seriously ... after we eat. In South Carolina, politics is sanctified.

But breakfast? Breakfast is *imbued*.

After all, it's in the Constitution, isn't it? Life, liberty and the pursuit of a Happy Meal.

Anyway, in case you missed it, here's a handy recap of South Carolina's Presidential Primary Day 2012. The blow-by-blow, if you will, the way I saw it.

After breakfast.

7.00am
In polling places all across the state, several million TV news crews poise, countdown "three, two, one, roll tape!" and simultaneously point their cameras at ... nothing. A bunch of empty rooms.
Remember, it's Saturday morning, it's raining, and polling places don't offer coffee.

8.00am

At a rally in Columbia, Governor Nikki Haley strongly endorses Mitt Romney, citing the undisputable fact that both their last names end in "ey." Former Governor Mark Sanford was scheduled to appear, but he misread his map and wound up at a Brazilian micro-brewery.

8.01am

Current President Barack Obama surges ahead of all other candidates in the Democrat primary, or would have done, if there *were* any other candidates in the Democrat primary.

The incumbent reacts by singing four notes of "Pretty Woman" from the third tee.

9.00am

A poll conducted by Clemson University shows Newt Gingrich holding a slight lead. This confuses university officials, who were not aware that the school even had a Department of Statistics. Clemson's arch-rivals at the University of South Carolina quickly respond by getting arrested for disorderly conduct.

10.00am

Due to a scheduling conflict, two Republican candidates show up, at the same time, at Tommy's Ham House in Greenville. The combined weight of the egos collapses the floor, injuring seven patrons and 42,000 sausage biscuits.

10.30am

Despite heavy rainfall, poll-watchers say that voter turnout is very high. And contrary to some reports, primary voters in South Carolina, after voting, are NOT given stickers saying "I Done Voted."

That's what happens in *North* Carolina.

11.00am

Responding to a 'conspiracy theory' heckler at a Political Christian Scientist Monitor Versus Merrimack rally in Charleston, incumbent Barack Obama officially denies that he has ever been to Mars.

Ron Paul immediately demands that we withdraw our troops from Fort Sumter.

11.30am

Mitt Romney points out that "newt" is a synonym for "salamander." Newt Gingrich fires back that Mitt's first name is Willard, the name of a movie about a boy who likes rats.

Ron Paul immediately demands that we withdraw our troops from Hollywood.

12.00pm

At noon today, all across the state, political rallies are interrupted by hordes of car dealers wearing big hair and bad suits. A spokesman for the group, Jim "Jim" Gallstone of Cotton Mather Motor Sales, defends the bold action, pointing out that since candidates had bought up all the available ad time, this was the only way car dealers could get on TV to advertise their last sale ever, until next week's last sale ever.

1.00pm

In a taped message from his bus, on his plane, on the way to a golf vacation, incumbent Barack Obama documents his qualifications by singing - *FROM MEMORY* - seven notes from

"Mama Said" by The Shirelles. The crowd goes wild, and four women went into spontaneous labor.

1.45pm

During a debate at a Rock Hill diner, CNN moderator John "Larry" King presses Newt Gingrich to explain Newt's choice of mustard-based, rather than tomato-based barbecue sauce. A deeply-offended Gingrich electrifies the BBQ-buffet lunch crowd, firing back that barbecue sauce is a deeply personal decision; plus, the biased national media wouldn't know a pepper-rubbed flank from a Boston Butt.

CNN offers a butt-rub rebuttal, but I've already gone way too far with this joke.

2.00pm

A pundit points out that, for over 30 years, South Carolina has correctly picked the eventual Republican candidate, calling the state "kind of a litmus test for the South." The SC Department of Education immediately schedules a "Teacher Work Day" so students can study, in case they need to take a litmus test.

2.30pm

At an Upstate rally, Newt notes all the young people in attendance. He points out that he's always glad to see young people getting involved in politics, particularly that one hottie over there wearing the 'Scooter's Exotic-Like Pole Dancing & Lunch Buffet' t-shirt.

Ron Paul immediately demands that we withdraw our troops from downtown Bangkok.

3.00pm

An MSNBC reporter in Myrtle Beach calls South Carolinians a bunch of gun-toting religious rednecks. The Greater Grand Strand Women's Auxiliary Gospel Choir And Transmission Repair Shop scoffed at the characterization, and then shot him.

3.30pm

In an announcement surprising on several levels, South Carolina's premier religious radio station (WASP) endorses The Shirelles for President. The endorsement comes from the station's chaplain, a heavily-jowled AARP member with a Pentagon-sized pomade allowance.

During the station's call-in segment, Al Gore claims that he invented Motown.

Ron Paul immediately demands that we withdraw Newt Gingrich from The Shirelles.

4.30pm

At a rally near North Charleston, GOP candidate Brick Sanitarium is injured after being gang-swarmed by adoring, sweater-vest-clad freshmen from Pinewood Prep School.

Incumbent Barack Obama immediately waives the freshmen's student loans.

5.00pm

At a rally near Augusta National golf course, Ron Paul is interrupted by incumbent incompetent Joe Biden, who inexplicably yells "Go Giants!" and almost doesn't swear.

Suddenly, Jackie Chan pops out of a water hazard, throat-chops Biden, and replaces Ron Paul's iced tea with a V-8 Smoothie.

5.05pm

Local evening news leads with the breaking story that candidate Gingrich has, not three, but several dozen ex-wives. A Gingrich spokesman denies the allegation, but points out that Newt *is* the "family values" candidate, so the more families, the better.

6.00pm

Mike Huckabee, FoxNews' official bass guitar analyst, points out that incumbent Barack Obama, in his first term as President, never once finished an entire song.

Due to a serious breach in security, Joe Biden manages to find an open mike and inexplicably promises federal subsidies for Hilton Head, so they can build more high-rise condoms.

6.55pm

Geraldo Rivera, desperate to inject himself in this humor column before 7.00pm, claims that, while covering a story in Aruba, he and Hillary Clinton had been shot at by Chechnyan rebels, and Jackie Chan.

7.01pm

The South Carolina polls are closed, and I couldn't be happier, because all during this column I kept forgetting to write in the present tense.

Presidential Primary Day ends without incident. Nobody voted for Pat Buchanan by mistake.

Out of pure habit, Al Gore challenges the election.

And Ron Paul immediately demands that we withdraw medication from Al Gore.

.

What *is* a Hustings, Anyway?

(Some notes on Stupor Tuesday...and beyond)

Last weekend I went to an oyster roast, a yearly fundraiser held in my home town. It was an excellent evening, with family, good friends, live music and great food. And a great opportunity to take a much-needed break from American politics.

Right...

The oysters were flown in from the coast of Mississippi. And at one point during the evening, I grabbed a freshly-steamed oyster from the nearest bucket, used my nubby little knife to pry it open, and saw a tiny campaign poster from Mitt Romney.

Unless you're dead, or watching American Idol, you may have noticed an ongoing Presidential election campaign. (Here in my home state of South Carolina, even if you are dead, you can still vote. And buy a gun. After all, there's a reason half of Charleston is haunted.)

215

American politicians. The ultimate used-car salesmen, but with one major difference - politicians never paid for the cars they're trying to sell you.

And now America has just come through one of the more odd highlights of every campaign season: Super Tuesday. This is a day when ten (eleven?) states vote (or caucus) to designate delegates (which may or may not be binding) for Presidential candidates (if their paperwork is in order). It's like some kind of low-budget, fast-paced caper flick, starring expensive haircuts grafted on to grinning rich people.

I still haven't figured out if Wyoming is included in Super Tuesday. I'm told there are ten states involved, not counting Wyoming. But on Super Tuesday, people in Wyoming are voting on something, and Wyoming makes eleven. Apparently, the political pundits have even figured out alternative ways to count to ten.

You may not know it, especially if you went to public school, or are watching American Idol, but Wyoming has a rich history. Wyoming is the only territory granted statehood solely due to having lots of potential hamburgers. Wyoming, as a voting bloc, has more cows than voters; in fact, there are more cows in Wyoming than there are cows in India, even though we eat ours. (our cows, not our out-sourced computer help desks)

But either way, when compared to delegate-rich political plums like California and Texas, Wyoming is unfairly ignored. Wyoming only wields something like three delegate votes (five, if you weigh them on the hoof).

Anyway - here we are, in March 2012, a Mayan-calendar-expiration election-season end-of-the-world leap year (whew - talk about 'March Madness!'). End-of-time prophets are selling short. Rogue solar flares are threatening to disrupt smart-phone communications, which could result in citizens having to count, remember appointments, and speak directly to each other. All over facebook, people are talking about brooms that apparently can stand up without assistance, and a Georgetown law-school coed that apparently can't.

And the 2012 campaign, which actually began around 7:01pm, 4 November 2008, is in full swing. The candidates are, as the expression goes, out on the hustings. It's a gargantuan, obscene and obscenely expensive exercise in comparison shopping.

See, right there is a clue. This candidate has fewer miles, but that one is safer. Could be ten elections today, could be eleven. All of them count, or not, depending. But check out those floor mats! The whole thing reeks of used car.

But the Washington wannabes continue to bustle about the countryside, smiling and frowning, explaining and complaining, balking and talking, weaving, waving and wavering.

And no matter what the topic, no matter how irrelevant the news item, political pundits will find a way to work it in to the story - with a negative slant, if at all possible.

Here are some sample Super Tuesday state-by-state snapshots:

Georgia

- Newt Gingrich appears to have won Georgia.
- Mitt Romney appears to have purchased Georgia.
- Herman Cain has been accused of dating Georgia.
- Bill Maher called Georgia a slut.
- And President Obama, at a $8-billion-a-plate fundraiser, sang nine notes from "Georgia."

Vermont

- Mitt Romney was expected to have won Vermont.
- Ron Paul was checking the price of gold and drove right past Vermont.
- Ethan Allen, the founder of Vermont, was pardoned by Bill Clinton.
- Rick Santorum pointed out that Mitt Romney's name can be rearranged to spell "Memory Tint," after which Santorum was given a calming medication.
- And Rush Limbaugh called Ethan Allen a slut.

Oklahoma

- Rick Santorum looks to have won Oklahoma.
- Mitt Romney looks to have purchased front row seats to the musical "Oklahoma."
- Joe Biden pointed out that Tulsa spelled backwards "a slut."
- Rick Santorum accused Joe Biden of chanting words backwards within 100 feet of a church.
- And President Obama promised 666 congaskillion dollars to General Motors for their new crossover

vehicle, "The Solar-Powered Surrey with the Fringe Benefits On Top."

By the way - I don't know what a hustings is or are, but whatever it or they may be, if you take your cues from the news, you can be sure of several things:

- Mitt Romney will have several
- Rick Santorum will be the only candidate with *true* hustings
- Newt Gingrich will know its definition, three synonyms, and will have regularly discussed the topic with Reagan
- Ron Paul will be strongly against America's presence in the hustings
- And President Obama will expect you give your hard-earned hustings to somebody else who doesn't have so many

So, get out there and vote! If you're dead, vote anyway!

And if you vote for our candidate, we'll throw in the floor mats.

Fifty Grand for Tale-Gunner Joe

(All States were created equal. All statesmen were not.)

Lately, it seems that some of America's fifty States are competing to deliver the most bizarre news imaginable. And, admittedly, it's a tight race to the bottom.

If you're a news junkie, that's great. But if you're a student of humanity, or a mid-level pan-Galactic deity charged with Milky Way Moron Management, it can get a bit depressing.

Americans just keep trying to out-stupid each other. And that was *before* Joe Biden started running around the country, lobbing non-sequiturs and spouting gaffes like some kind of political poster child for Tourette's.

But the news "gatekeepers" always focus on the same States; California, Arizona, New York, Mexico, the Kennedy compound, the Land of Loco Starlets. We rarely get a glimpse at the goings-on in the engine of America - that vast mass rudely referred to as "the flyover States."

221

Surely, we wondered, the flyover States are just as goofy.

So, for your edification, we've corralled our entire global research staff, and asked her to check out what's making news across *all* our fifty states. Witness:

Alabama
The "Yellowhammer" State continues to push for the toughest immigration laws in the country, including the mandate that any school child can be stopped and forced to compose a limerick using the word "yellowhammer."
By the way, we should note that Alabama has a State Nut.

Alaska
An undecided moose allegedly survived being stabbed in the thigh by Sarah Palin. Later, at a quail hunt, the hapless moose was shot in its alpha antler by Dick Cheney. Ultimately, the moose succumbed to all this political pressure, joined the Tea Party, and was elected Governor. Liberal news organizations immediately put tactical teams in the area, located the moose's nightly resting tree, and rented the tree next door.

Arizona
Headline: *Man Shot By Albuquerque Cops High On Meth*
All right. Who's giving guns to doped-up cops?

Arkansas
Anthropologists claim to have discovered an anomaly - a human female that Bill Clinton never hit on. Lack-of-paternity test results are pending. (These are scientists from the University's

satellite campus in Cecil, down along the State Road 16 Spur, over there nearby to the Sonic.)

This just in: never mind.

California

In the Golden State, they have earthquakes, tar pits and TV executives. Feral coyotes and financing by the kilo. City employees getting taxpayer-funded sex changes, with seven official genders to choose from. Businesses fleeing like Hamelin rats. Air the consistency of loaf bread. And a governor whose job resume highlight was being a liquid-metal android from the future that managed to make sequels *after* it died. *Twice.*

So what draws the Fed's focus?

Medicinal marijuana.

Colorado

Speaking at a fundraiser in Beulah, Joe Biden warned a group of disaffected Buddhist donors that if those vile Republicans block the President's agenda, more women will be raped. The White House was quick to point out that this would save or create millions of jobs for sexual deviants, or Congressmen.

Connecticut

Our research staff tried to rouse someone in the Constitution State, but they're all busy trying to fend off a hostile takeover by New York City. The Big Apple's looking to annex Connecticut, erect parking garages, and have it renamed "Brooklyn North."

Delaware

Delaware continues to make news as the only state that's actually building a border fence. However, in Delaware's case, they're building it in hopes of keeping Joe Biden from getting back in.

Florida

A lawmaker in the Sunshine State wants to do away with Florida's ban on dwarf tossing. That's just so...well, so *Florida*. Firstly, there's an activity in Florida called dwarf tossing. Secondly, it's wildly popular. Next, naturally, Florida's legislature outlaws it. And finally, a grass-roots movement to repeal the anti-dwarf-tossing legislation.

So Florida. I mean, let's face it - there never was any need, really, to discuss where to put Disney World. It was kismet.

Georgia

Headline: *SLED Director Lays Out Agency's Mission*

Sheesh. That director's got some temper. Wonder what the mission said?

Hawaii

Aloha! (literal translation: "Please leave before you get here, if not sooner") Hawaii is perhaps best known as being one of the three birthplaces of President Barack Obama.

Idaho

In the Gem State, a body was found in the Kuna reservoir, another in an Ada County canal, and a car dinged a teenager on Lake (*LAKE?*) Lowell Avenue - *on the same day*. In an unsolicited speech to himself, Joe Biden insisted that patriotic taxpayers should bail out stuff that's wet, and assigned blame to all those damp Republicans.

Illinois

Officials in Des Plaines had to call in extra help to deal with a sharp spike in the skunk population. The skunk count blip is variously blamed on either a rise in the beetle grub population, a drop in rabies, or the recent installation of Rahm Emanuel as Mayor of Chicago.

Indiana

Headline: *Missing Student's Mom Hurt By Letter*
Note to Missing Student's Mom: When you see a letter coming, duck.

Iowa

In an attempt to bolster out-of-state attendance to their famous State Fairs, Iowa unveiled eleven more unlikely things that could be deep-fried.

Kansas

In a first-of-its-kind legal action, Kansas (the State) is suing Kansas (the band). Kansas (State) is demanding that the 1970s rockers officially change their name to some other State. Nebraska was highly recommended, but so was Detroit, which says a lot about the state of public education in Kansas.

Kentucky

A Lexington drifter was sentenced to twenty-five and one-half years in prison: twenty-five years for committing violent crimes, another six months for contempt ("lifting his middle finger").

The transient's other nine fingers immediately filed a digit discrimination counter-suit, and are being represented by celebrity attorney Gloria Allred.

Louisiana
According to a Pelican State news website named "The Dead Pelican" (really, that's what it's named), a Shreveport robbery went awry when one of the intruders mistakenly shot the other one. Then the police arrived, everybody arrested each other, and the entire group was given a nice set of abandoned FEMA house trailers.

Maine
Residents were saddened when yet another research grant failed to ascertain why Maine is still known as "down East."

Maryland
This morning, while speaking at a "Re-elect Us Anyway" fundraiser, Joe Biden warned that if those vile Republicans block the President's agenda, all college football teams would morph into rabid dogs and eat everybody in the stadium.
The White House was quick to claim a bipartisan victory, pointing out that the rabid dogs would eat everybody equally. (Plus, the White House noted, Joe got through three consecutive sentences without swearing.)

Massachusetts
Our research staff tried to rouse someone in the Bay State, but the entire state government had been mobilized to deal with a Mitt Romney hair emergency.

Michigan

In Detroit, the ACLU legally challenged an FBI sting operation. That, of course, hardly qualifies as news. What *is* news is that, this time, the FBI finally told the ACLU to shut up and sit down.

Minnesota

Headline: *Minneapolis Metro Transit Rides Hit 60 Million*

60 million hit by metro transit? We're guessing that the ACLU and celebrity attorney Gloria Allred are racing toward the North Star State as we speak.

Mississippi

After uncovering one Pulitzer-worthy headline from a Magnolia State news website, our research staff had a decision to make. The headline? "Fun With Worms."

Nah.

Moving on to Missouri...

Missouri

In a story about zoning issues, we found this bizarre observation: "Officials blamed [the problem] on lack of red tape." We're not sure that those words have ever been uttered, in that order, in the history of Earth.

Montana

An environmentalist coalition in the Treasure State is pleased to announce they are making progress in their legal efforts to ban roads. No word on their pending legislation to outlaw light.

Nebraska

Citizens in the Cornhusker State are embroiled in a debate about someone who dug a three-foot hole in something called the Ogallala Aquifer. And it's just such levels of rural ennui that explain Al Gore's rush to pipe in internet access to backwaters like Ogallala as soon as humanly possible.

Nevada

A member of the Hells Angels who was supposedly killed at the funeral of a member of the Hells Angels who was killed during the killing of a former member of the Hells Angels has been discovered alive by the police who were not killed by the members of the Hells Angels who were not killed during the killing of an ousted member of the Hells Angels. Meanwhile, no word on the missing possessive apostrophe from "Hells Angels."

New Hampshire

Three New Hampshire citizens were playing poker in a Delaware hotel when three more fun-lovers barged in and started pistol-slapping the room's original occupants. The assailants ran away when the bedside phone received an "Are you injured?" robo-call from celebrity attorney Gloria Allred. Hard-line NH secessionists pointed out that this kind of vile activity would never have happened in Old Hampshire.

New Jersey

A Garden State resident (Hackettstown turnpike exit) who was served divorce papers in 1992 (filed at a Hackensack turnpike exit) has been convicted of watching helplessly, with malice aforethought, while his wife tied herself up, gagged herself, and jumped backwards off a cliff (Palisades turnpike exit). But hey, that's New Jersey, yo.

New Mexico
While speaking to a roomful of semi-conscious turquoise jewelry artisans, Joe Biden claimed that he had inherited Muammar Qaddafi from George W. Bush. Undergrads at a local dentistry college offered to volunteer their services to have Biden's teeth filed down before he hurts himself.

New York
A single woman and her single grandmother have created a blog, to share their experiences in the cyber-world of online dating. According to Granny, what's the most important characteristic of a Senior Citizen single guy?
  1) He's honest
  2) He has a sense of humor
  3) He lives nearby

North Carolina
During a Homeland Security speech in Raleigh, Janet Napolitano was asked a question by someone in the audience who admitted - *admitted* - he was in the country illegally. Napolitano lunged so violently for a "Border Arrests Are Up" chart that she pulled a muscle in an Arizona rancher's back. Celebrity attorney Gloria Allred immediately arranged for the illegal to get in-state tuition and free health care.

North Dakota
The president of Dickinson State University says he's innocent of tampering with enrollment records. He further claims that stress

related to the unfounded accusations resulted in him losing twenty-five pounds, which in turn caused him to eat all the subpoenaed documents.

Ohio

A deranged Buckeye apparently heard some voice inside his skull that told him the rains were receding, so he should go ahead and let all the animals out of the ark. Here's the scary part: no candidate has ever become President without winning over Ohio voters. And if this guy was an example of an Ohio voter...

Oklahoma

According to a news report, the police chief in Mangum was accused of getting in a fight at a rodeo in Altus after his stepdaughter didn't get voted Rodeo Princess. Punctuating the story is *this* shocker: the chief was intoxicated at the time.

We should note that, in Oklahoma, these are the *good* guys.

Oregon

At a building dedication in Portland, former Senator Margaret Carter stole the show, but after lunch, she brought it back. Charges may still be filed, however, according to celebrity attorney Gloria Allred, who refused to comment on her comment, since she's representing both sides, and the lunch.

Pennsylvania

Our staff uncovered one headline from a Keystone State news website that read: "Hershey Trojans break under pressure."

And our staff realizes that there are times when we need to just move away from the joke.

Rhode Island
Due to new FCC regulations, the Ocean State has been classified a virtual State (a Statelet), resulting in them having to relinquish their static IP address and set up some kind of interstate internet router sharing with the larger, full-sized States next door.

South Carolina
Headline: *City Adds Streets To Road Repaving List*
Clever lads. Wonder what they were paving before they thought of streets? Next thing you know, they may start putting police in the Police Department and adding water to the water.

South Dakota
Our research staff tried to rouse someone in the Mount Rushmore State, but we kept getting a recording that both circuits were busy.

Tennessee
During our research for this article, Libya's Qaddafi was finally captured by a French drone funded by American taxpayer money borrowed from Chinese banks to support President Obama's not-war. Speaking at Dollywood to a group of plus-sized Lacrosse Moms who collect commemorative railroad plates, Joe Biden cited this as a White House victory that will clearly reduce violence against non-conservative women.

Texas
Our research staff tried to rouse someone in the Lone Star State, but we were unable to hear anything over the erratic gunfire, wailing harmonicas, and official Rick Perry retractions.

Utah

We can't share the top news from Utah, because our news contact in the Beehive State has five wives and they're still arguing over what the top news is.

Vermont

Vermont is struggling with the recent discovery that it's really nothing more than a chunk of upstate New York, shaped like a flipped-over New Hampshire. Apparently, in the late 1700s, "Vermont" was sold to a western New Hampshire land baron by a traveling jigsaw puzzle salesman.

Virginia

I don't know why, but an Old Dominion State news website posted an entire article on how to pronounce stuff. The "stuff" included a long 'a,' the letter 'k,' a judge named 'Leonie Brinkema' and a potential ACLU client named 'Abdelhaleem Hasan Abdelraziq Ashqar.'

Washington

In the Evergreen State, proposed legislation intends to limit humans to 3 emergency room visits per year, but there are reams of legalese in place to protect trees. Basically, in Washington, lumber is treated more humanely than lumberjacks.

West Virginia

West Virginia has a request. For a little while, for kicks, they would like to be called "East Kentucky." Just for kicks. Just for a little while.

Wisconsin

Nothing much is happening in Wisconsin, because the entire population have unionized and are holed up in a Rockford, Illinois motel.

Wyoming

There's a state named Wyoming?

Till Debt Do Us Part

(Congress. Casey. Zombies. Czars. Lemonade. Only in America.)

The good news is the zombie invasion is over. The bad news is the Casey Anthony invasion is just getting started.

We'd have been better off with the zombies.

To be sure, I never saw it coming. But then, nobody else saw it coming, either. America still boasts legions of smart people, but they're all unemployed. We still have hordes of geniuses with a knack for de-complicating complex clues and discerning underlying patterns in chaos, like those pale, oddly-dressed clerks whose job it is to sit in dark cubicles and calculate your cable bill. But this year, all those smart people are out on the streets, fighting for the same six jobs sorting bolts at the local hardware store.

What we needed was a dedicated, focused, brain-intensive agency, along the lines of our bygone heroes, SETI (Search for Entertaining Television Idols) and NASA (Nee A Space Agency).

235

It's been a tough year to have brains. SETI, whose grand mission was to search for signs of intelligent life, stubbornly stuck to its agenda despite having a budget smaller than your average fifth-grader's illegal lemonade stand. But one slow weekend at the lab, somebody flipped the channel over to coverage of the Casey Anthony trial, and the "search for intelligent life" futility sunk in. Overwhelmed by the irony of it all, SETI giggled itself to death.

NASA, meanwhile, wrapped up three decades of miracles known as the Space Shuttle program and was rewarded for its efforts by having its utilities disconnected. NASA couldn't contribute to solving the zombie problem; our ex-NASA scientists have been relegated to scribbling at Sudoku while standing in line for their unemployment checks. They're hunkered down at home, hording MREs and Tang. Consider their history:

President Kennedy: NASA goes to the moon.
President Reagan: NASA builds a space station.
President Obama: NASA loses 18,000 jobs, is forced to scrabble up beer money by holding Muslim self-actualization seminars, and has to call Russia every time they need a ride to the store.

But now that the zombie crisis has passed, let's take a minute to point out some of the players, and review some of the clues that took us to the brink of disaster. Witness:

- According to facts, decades of obscene spending finally caught up with Washington. According to Washington, somebody snuck into Congress' bedroom and stole all its money. According to Congress, America ran into a totally unexpected debt crisis because Wall Street rolled such a low number that we didn't pass "GO" and collect 200 (trillion) dollars. Outraged fingers pointed everywhere (else), fixing blame on everyone (else), including Republicans, Democrats, a Tea Party, a Tupperware Party, that little mustached guy from Monopoly, and George Bush.

- Meanwhile, in an Orlando television recording stu...I mean, uh, courtroom, a Florida mother with fabulous teeth was acquitted of murder and other crimes when the defense proved that the deeds were actually committed by an imaginary Latino woman, and George Bush. Then, just after midnight, Casey Anthony and her teeth got out of prison. For some reason, this made her staggeringly famous, prompting television crews to track her every move, up to and including follicle activity and the generation of internal enzymes. Within an hour, she had inked a deal to star in a new TV show, "Dancing with America's Most Wanted."

- The President flew to St. Louis and warned that he had to raise taxes (although he didn't want to); otherwise, there could be a horrible invasion of flesh-eating zombies, or worse, Republicans.

- As America's debt limit deadline loomed, America's leadership took charge, as evidenced by a Republican, sitting next to the playground window, who shot a spitball across the classroom at a Democrat. The world financial markets cautiously gauged these mixed signals.

- The President flew to Tucson and warned that the Tea Party had been selling lemonade, and stockpiling a zombie army, without a license.

- Casey Anthony was spotted at the grand opening of a tattoo parlor in northern Georgia, where she selflessly offered to auction off her imagination to charity.

- During a Texas Hold-Em game, Congress-person Sheila Jackson Lee held up a race card and began to speak to the press, but suddenly her hair collapsed, killing nine.

- As America's debt limit deadline loomed, the President warned that America's debt limit deadline was looming.

- Casey Anthony was spotted at an Omaha diner, eating a waffle that, according to locals, is the spitting image of Saint Patrick. No, wait. That was Elvis.

- The President flew to Cleveland and warned that we only had a few days left, before the Tea Party started beheading everybody's Grandma and Republicans began cross-channeling toxic waste pipes into the national water supply. Sales of zombie-piercing bullets skyrocketed.

- Casey Anthony accused a fictitious babysitter of showing up at her fictitious job and kidnapping her fictitious boyfriend. Alert officers questioned her testimony after she signed her name as "George Bush." Celebrity attorney Gloria Allred cited a "reality bias" and agreed to represent any and all people that don't exist.

- Vice President Joe Biden gave an inspiring, profanity-laced commencement speech, pointing out that he'd managed to attain the office of Vice President despite his inability to grasp the simple concept of "open mike." Unfortunately, he had misread his daily schedule and gave the commencement speech to a roomful of undocumented eight-year-olds awaiting extradition for lemonade misdemeanors.

- The President flew to Baltimore and signed an executive order granting in-state tuition to undocumented flesh-eating zombies.

- As America's debt limit deadline loomed, a Democrat dipped a Republican's pigtail in an inkwell, and had to stay after class and write on the blackboard, 100 times, "I promise not to limit debate pertaining to the revenue-neutral out-years posited among any caucus during non-binding participatory proscriptive abrogation in the well of the Senate, or the lower intestine of the House, by invoking an obscure Title Nine parliamentary cloture, and I promise, each day, to floss."

- Flesh-eating zombies were sighted outside a casino in Vegas. No, wait. That was Elvis.

- Congress-person Sheila Jackson Lee introduced a bill decrying the entire Universe as racist, pointing out the obvious: there are no cosmic anomalies known as "white holes."

- The President flew to Dallas, read a speech, smiled, waved and nodded knowingly. Joe Biden cursed for a while and then attended a ball game, where he misread his daily briefing and tried to lead the crowd in a heat wave.

- As America's debt limit deadline loomed, a Democrat made a face at a Republican during Science class. The Republican responded by passing a folded note across the classroom that read, "U R a big stupid."

- While initiating a tax audit on a Bethesda lemonade stand, Nancy Pelosi frightened a crowd of small children and was arrested for grinning without a license.

- Congress-person Sheila Jackson Lee accused Bing Crosby of racism for his obviously intolerant rendition of "White Christmas." In a related story, the ACLU sued Bing Crosby for forcing the word "Christmas" on unsuspecting mall shoppers.

- The President flew to Philadelphia and alleged that the Liberty Bell had been deliberately cracked by George Bush. He then warned senior citizens that Republicans wanted to take away their right to claim being killed more than once by a flesh-eating zombie as a "pre-existing condition."

- The Cesar Chavez Memorial Orchard-Workers Union (Bing Cherries Local 411) sued Bing Crosby for copyright infringement. Undocumented zombie field laborers picketed, petitioning for universal post-mortem health coverage.

- Casey Anthony was spotted at a Zombie Victim Anger Management seminar wearing nothing but a tattoo and a hat made of duct tape. No, wait. That was Joe Biden.

And then, in the eleventh hour, Treasury Secretary Tim Geithner had a brilliant idea. He held a brief conference with Casey

Anthony and then drove her up to the US Treasury, where she assumed all of America's debt. Then, thirty minutes later, she plea-bargained, and all the debt was forgiven.

America was saved!

The President took credit for the victory, then flew somewhere and read something. Democrats claimed victory, took up a donation, and bought dinner. Republicans claimed victory, took up a donation, and bought a restaurant. A local food workers union made a donation to each, claimed a deduction for both, and bought a Senator.

Congress responded to the good news by drafting a non-binding resolution affirming their consistent, on-the-record support for news that is good. Then they named a post office after Casey Anthony, raised taxes, and took a month off.

The Tea Party sighed and continued with their rally, where their fanatical supporters continued to get caught on camera not being violent.

America, bored with watching television news coverage of the Casey Anthony story, went back to watching television talk show coverage of the Casey Anthony story.

And all the zombies slugged to a staggered halt, reversed course and began lurching back to the unholy darkness from whence they came: the ACLU.

Nolo Contendere (Tales of a Single Guy)

~*~*~

"The only difference between me and a madman is that I am not mad."

Salvador Dali

~*~*~*~*~

Full Frontal Stupidity

The Future King of Tonga

(How to abdicate a throne when you don't rule anything)

I give up.

Here's what it's come to. Here's how weird it's gotten, just to try and be a guy in America.

I'm in the parking lot at the grocery, right? I see a stranger approaching, a lady, juggling bags and produce and wallets and keys. I analyze her situation, I calculate my options, I react. I lean in to open the strange lady's car door. Just trying to help, right?

And she nun chucks me with her wrist-collar of plastic "Valued Customer" bonus cards.

Sheesh. I didn't realize she was *that* strange.

So I'm making it official.

I give up.

Being an American Guy has just gotten too confusing. I'm going gender-neutral, like Switzerland, or Jimmy Swaggart.

I don't know when the switch got flipped, but somehow the simple act of holding a door open for a female has morphed from "Why, thank you, polite, well-mannered fellow!" into "What's up with *that* freak?" Things were much different when I was growing up, back when there were only three TV channels and two genders. I was taught to stand up when a lady entered the room.

But should you dare to exhibit such psychotic behavior these days, get ready for askance stares - and not just from the acknowledged lady. From the other women in the room, too.

And the men. And the potted plants.

And no, I did not stand up because I considered her weak. No, I did not stand up because I thought she was inferior.

I stood up because I thought she was *HOT.* (Remember, I was growing up. At that point in my development, I thought the *potted plants* were hot.)

Now, before I start getting emails from irritated feminists, and offended Schefflera, let me point out that, statistically speaking, guys *are* idiots.

Yeah, I said it. Many guys *are* morons. This is a confirmed, repeated, measurable fact. I mean, look at us. Look at our historical record:

- Once upon a time, a guy launched a thousand ships because of a woman's face. This became the first documented practical joke in a long history of maritime pranks spawned by guys, grog, and "Fleet Week."

- In the 1500s, an Italian guy named Nat King Cole painted the portrait of Mona Lisa, immortalizing her inscrutably sly smile. This painting would later become all the rage in freshman-level art appreciation classes as being the first example of "perspective," though hardly the first example of "smirking."

- A guy who became a King in England insisted on marrying multiple women ... at the same time. After about two weeks of *that*, the breakfast bickering drove him insane - surprise, surprise - and he had no choice but to "cloister" them in London's infamous Leaning Tower of Babel.

- According to legend, a guy named Narcissus fell in love with his own reflection in a pond, even though his reflection was occasionally marred by surfacing turtles. For thousands of years, he was unable to tear himself away from himself, until the year 2008 AD, when he was elected President of the United States.

- Another bunch of guys, desperate to rout the USC Trojans, redefined military tactics by hiding inside a hollow horse next to Saddam Hussein. Not only did these guys think it was a good idea to carve a giant horse and then hide in it; the Other Evil Bad Guys actually fell for it, which is where we get the term "never look a gift horse in the mouth, especially if you hear guys' voices and clinking armor coming from inside the horse."

And this is no recent phenomenon, either. According to some tenured university scientists, the Earth is 4,600 million years old. (This is what is commonly referred to as a SWAG. Floating a SWAG is normal behavior for a guy. Tenure was created so women could do it, too.) But it was only about 15,000 years ago that guys started knuckle-walking across the Bering Straits, en route to Malibu and Laguna Beach, looking for babes with minimal facial hair.

See? Even four thousand million years ago, already guys were sleeping in, showing up late and, as it turns out, not all that picky.

So, to be fair, there is some validity to the "we're made that way" argument. And, as a matter of scientific objectivity, any time you run across a life form that spray-paints profane graffiti in block capital letters, but uses cursive to "write" its name in the snow, you definitely want to double-check the creature's DNA.

But, unlike tenured people, you have to check your sources. You can't just lump all guys into a single, single-celled-organism category. For example, guys in general are expected to know how to make quick, determined decisions, and how to fix stuff. Not true. I once borrowed a friend's late-model Saab and nearly died of dehydration before I figured out where to insert the ignition key.

And trust me. Somewhere out there, right now, is a guy with a weighty decision to make. Just a guy ... perhaps he's a rugged yet sympathetic high school sports coach, tall, balding, probably sporting a mild limp from a selfless accident during his pool lifeguard days. And every morning, this guy can be found standing in front of his open gym locker, staring at bottles of competing ibuprofen medications.

Should he take two of this one, or eight of that? Or did he already take a handful and forget? If so, which one? What if he took both? According to the TV commercials, either one could cause his heartbeat to stutter, or his ankles to dissolve. Either might cause him to drool, faint, or, according to some double-blind tests, go blind twice. Both might cause skin vomiting, nausea, queasiness or other synonyms. Neither should be taken while sleeping, or while not sleeping, or while scuba diving or not, or while operating monstrous machinery that third-world countries use to gouge out diamond quarries.

Ultimately, the upshot is that guys are expected to be a kind of social shape-shifter. Adaptable to the point of genetic de-differentiation. A set of men for all seasons.

All of whom, it is readily assumed, are bone-banging stupid.

As a guy, I can absolutely assure you of one thing: no guy wakes up of a morning, eager to run outside and compete for "Moron of the Year." But societal sources are forever at the ready, monitoring guys for any outbreak of *Pending Idiot Syndrome* ... and these sources never sleep. Including the most insidious source of all - television.

When it comes to TV, guys can't win. In the sports, shows, and specials, guys are depicted as everything from slime to saint; but in the commercials, it's all about the idiots.

Here's a partial list of TV commercial concepts that you, as a 21st Century Guy, are expected to do or accept, or tolerate, or embrace and understand, or defend against a Quentin Tarantino-sized squad of Ninja assassins, all while simultaneously flexing your six-pack abs, weeping at a Hugh Grant movie, and killing a spider:

- A guy must know how to choose the correct shaving products. Present a nice, close shave and women will go all National Geographic at you; show up stubbly and you get snubbed like Paris Hilton at a eunuch convention. Plus, according to TV, if you don't dab on the right gel, your entire jaw could catch on fire.

- As a single guy, you've been sleeping in the same bed, on the same mattress, since the War of 1812 (Odds are, on the same sheets, too, but let's not niggle). But now, your new bride wants a new mattress made out of something called Super Memory Ultra-Enzyme Tushie-Molding Hyper-Foam (not to be confused with shaving gel). It gets worse. She wants you to extend and relax on your side of the bed, posed in your favorite Hugh Hefner silks, while she jumps up and down on the mattress' eastern hemisphere, grinning like a lapsed eunuch at a Paris Hilton convention, and absolutely fascinated by an obstinate flute of red wine that refuses to spill.

- A guy might get a phone call from his neighbor, alerting the guy that his pre-teen son, instead of delivering the paper each morning, has been lobbing boxes of whole-grain breakfast cereal onto people's lawns. What to do? Is his son insane? Is the kid knocking off the local grocery? Could breakfast cereal distribution be a gateway drug leading to unlicensed lemonade stands?

- As a guy, you will eagerly drop over $300 on a new smart phone, simply because it is 4G, or has 5 Gs, or does whatever it is smart phones do with however many Gs are available in this galaxy, this week. You can rationalize the purchase because, according to the ad, the phone will turn into a lightning bolt that you can throw like a spear from your barn. (some barn assembly required, batteries and thunderbolt not included)

- To prove that a spray-on product can seal a leaky gutter, a guy will gang-spray a screen door, then replace the bottom of a rowboat with the screen door.

- As a formerly-single guy, to placate your wife (a nasal shrew who's beginning to sound more and more like Gladys Kravitz from *Bewitched*), you will agree on a $3,600 awning to shade a sad slab of concrete that cost nine bucks, a pitiful, 3-by-5 postage stamp of pavement that Gladys refers to as "the lanai."

So, the next time you see a guy fumbling his way through society, think twice before you judge him. Remember, he's missed nearly four billion years of charm school.

FOOTNOTE: The parking lot lady didn't actually hit me. But you already knew that, because you're reading this column, which

I'd have never written if she had actually hit me, because I'd have sued the edgy little shopper right down to her last lime, cleaned up in the personal injury lawsuit, and that'd be the last time you ever heard from *me*, because I would've relocated *in mid-sentence* to the Island of Tonga, where I would run for King.

Hmm. Wonder if anybody makes a 5G Tushie-Foam throne.

The Cobra, the Cougar & the Hippo

(Never trust anyone wearing a lab coat and six-inch stilettos)

This year, for the first time in years, I actually had a yearly physical.

Now, before I start getting e-hate "tsk-tsk" spam mail from aghast adults, school cafeteria dieticians and annoying nanny-state crusader groups, let me explain. I don't mean to say that I haven't been to see a doctor in years. I simply mean that, this year, I had a yearly checkup just once.

See, I have one of those doctors who insist on seeing her patients about twice a week, due to the fact that she cares deeply about her patients, and has a boat payment. But this year, I had seriously threatened her yacht mortgage by not showing up twice a month to gaily lob cash at her.

I had my reasons, thank you very much; for one thing, I'd spent much of the year battling an evil, bipolar corporate dwarf. I'd also spent a good chunk of the year dueling with a government-managed health insurance program named COBRA (the Completely Outrageous Bogus Rates Agency), which is based on the logical premise that the most efficient way to provide affordable health care is to model it after a reptile that spits.

Finally, though, came the battle I could not win. Drugs. My prescriptions ran out, so I had to run in and beg for more. I set aside a few hours, spent a few hours practicing my signature, and drove to the doctor's.

At the doctor's window, I paid silent homage to the quantum advances in computerized medical technology by signing my name on a clipboard. A lady wearing a Flintstone-cartoon smock handed me a different clipboard, this one burdened with about an inch of federally-mandated forms. She pointed to a chair, directed me to fill out all the forms, and said she hoped I'd been practicing my signature.

One of these forms had been designed by some sadistic, sub-level bureaucratic optimist who actually expected me to fill out my name five times - on the same form:

1. Me, the patient
2. Me, the insured
3. Me, the owner of the insured's insurance
4. Me, the person filling out the form on behalf of Me, the patient and Me, the insured
5. Me, the person signing the form on behalf of the other four Mes

(And I'll bet you five bucks that, somewhere in some government building, there are five departments, with five budgets, five directors, and five staffs, each responsible for reading one of my five names.)

One form was particularly odd. Something about a hippo, though the clever claque spelled it HIPAA. Other than wanting my signature and today's date at the bottom, I have no idea what it was after. There were, maybe, seventeen-hundred paragraphs of legal-speak, written in some subatomic font, that seemed to be asking for my permission to let the doctor run around in public places, broadcasting my height and other closely-guarded medical secrets.

Several hours later, I finished the paperwork, applied for disability (writer's cramp), and was ushered back to the labyrinth to be weighed, which would either confirm or nullify my "hippo" paperwork.

After it was confirmed that I did, in fact, have weight, I sat in an examining room for a time, while another Flintstone smock ran through a scripted sequence of pushes, pokes, pricks, prods, squeezes, daubs and queries. It was like pledging a particularly picky fraternity, but without the beer.

And, finally, just before midnight, my doctor popped in, wearing a lab coat, open-toed high heels, and a foul-weather jacket. I couldn't tell if she'd showed to read my chart, or to christen a new aircraft carrier.

She proceeded to complain that one of my "numbers" was high, a potentially fatal medical condition caused by not having yearly physicals twice a month.

"See what happens when you miss an appointment?" she teased, as she logged on to the internet to check the outgoing tide tables. I threatened to hit her with some of my weight.

What was *that* about? Surely, she didn't expect me to believe there was some medical cause-and-effect relationship between my office visits and my internal vitals?

Was my doctor hitting on me? Or were she and her yacht simply chasing after my co-pay?

After sharing the bad numbers news, my doctor consulted a well-thumbed copy of the famous medical bible known as the PDR (Physicians' Deep-sea Reference). She spotted and circled an expensive fish-finding sonar, causing her to notice that I hadn't had an EKG in two years, and so I simply had to have one today, else my spleen could explode on a freeway on-ramp.

I tried to point out that EKGs weren't covered by my Hippo *or* my Cobra, but I was too late. Her eyes were already glazed over. She coveted the sonar, and she was not to be denied. She handed me one of those dreaded examining room gowns and instructed me to put it on, but with an unexpected twist - I was to leave the gown open in the front.

And now, I'll admit, I was troubled. Cautious. I had definite misgivings about submitting to my doctor's request for an EKG, for four very good reasons:

1. She, and others in her profession, insist on spelling "cardio" with a K
2. I wasn't just wearing one of their gowns - I was wearing one of their gowns *backwards*
3. She had referred to the EKG as a "prophylactic" procedure
4. She was wearing open-toed heels

So I bailed.

I jettisoned the exam gown, shoveled into my street clothes, scrambled for the exit and screamed out of the parking lot.

I don't know what consequences might ensue, but I'll worry about that next year.

Unless Doctor Cougar invites me and my gown to have a moonlit EKG on her yacht.

Full Frontal Stupidity

Rocky's Run for the Border

(Communing with nature, but with a dash of vengeance)

Somewhere, beyond the tree line that snakes along behind my house, there lives a lovely little female, a red-tailed fox, with a unique perk. This may be the only four-legged forager in America that can order in.

For the few years I've lived here, that fortunate fox has feasted on all my discards, all the pounds of food that an average single guy just can't ever seem to finish prior to the various expiration dates. Several times a week, I'd be out on my deck, lobbing groceries out at the green edge of (sic) civilization: sliced bread, sliced cheese. Buns that shouldn't be hard and veggies that should. Bagels with a pedigree that would have to be measured in half-lives. The occasional doggie-bagged dessert, the one-day-too-long pizza slice, the A Fridge Too Far fetid egg or fuzzy chop meat. Those weird little mutant miniature corn cobs that keep dropping out of the Universe and landing in my Chinese food.

And the little vixen never seemed to mind that she's getting my hand-me-downs. I suppose that's one of the advantages of being a feral female, along with the money you'd save on table silver. If you're the type of woman that can eat a live mouse, you're hardly likely to haughtily sniff at day-old Triscuits.

Lately, though, I haven't seen her around much, and now I know why. She's been dining in. Madame Fox no longer needs to pop over to Barry's Backyard Bakery & Ballast Disposal. Thanks to modern technology, mice are now just queuing up at her front porch and conveniently exploding.

Now you may think I'm lying, because I do that a lot, though only when I'm writing, or talking, or making hand gestures. But this "Mouse as Bottle Rocket" anecdote is knowledge I picked up directly from my friendly pest control person. You know him: this is that white-uniformed guy who pops in every other month and walks around the house, armed with a hose attached to a metal cylinder, and acts like he's spraying stuff, which may or may not be some invisible but monstrously toxic Bug Elimination Mist that I'm afraid of because I can't see it or smell it. Eventually, he'll finish his rounds, smile, hand me an old mimeographed copy of something that, for all I know, describes my liabilities regarding the Louisiana Purchase, and then something automagically debits my credit card.

But what Beau Peste shared with me is this: to ensure that I have no infestation of rodents, he's installed a little black brick of mice bait beneath my house. Here's the strategy: whenever some extraordinarily stupid or intensely bored mouse decides (for whatever rodent-oriented reason) to bite the brick, said mouse ingests the bait, prances along into the tree line and, ultimately, blows up.

You know ... for a humorist, reality's just a big, endless gift, isn't it?

So, obviously, my vixen-y neighbor now has it made. The evening's main course just shows up and blows up - heck, these entrees even self-filet. Milady fox just sits by the stream, humming and knitting little kit booties, watching Fox News, and waiting to hear that familiar popping noise.

You may be thinking, "Mouse parts. Now that's a nasty diet." And you may be right. Or you may be humbled into shut-up-ed-ness by two words: Hot Pockets.

Cast the first stone, biped.

Another example of the difference in dining habits between two- and four-legged fauna is the squirrel (*Scarfus maximus*). I have many squirrels frequenting my back yard, because I own a bird feeder, which is apparently a device you buy in order to feed squirrels.

See, I thought I bought my *bird* feeder to hold *bird* food, which I buy in 10-pound bags that have pictures of *birds* on the bag, and which I take home and pour into the *bird* feeder, in order to attract *birds*, who will happily eat the *bird* food and then thank me, in that cute *bird*-like way of theirs, by decorating my deck with staggering amounts of ex-*bird* stuff that is basically the *bird* equivalent of a political speech.

Ha. Shows you what little I know. Squirrels showed up at my bird feeder faster than Gloria Allred spotting a neurotic celebrity.

I buy bird feed, I get squirrels. I can't imagine what kind of lawn guests I'd have if I'd brought home some actual *squirrel* food and laid it around for free. Jackals, maybe, or Obama's economic team. (Yeah, I know they are.)

Now, don't get me wrong. I don't have anything against squirrels, structurally. True, they're basically rats that can climb trees, but that's not *their* fault. If you want to file a design complaint, you need to go take it up with the creator of the squirrel: Al Gore.

It's not the *fact* of the squirrel. It's their *attitude*. Squirrels have a right to eat, just like the rest of Al Gore's creatures. But I've watched these selfish little squirrels, these four-legged, entitlement-minded buffet boars. They'll grasp the side of my deck with their rear claws, hang upside down, and eat for twenty-nine consecutive days. They don't even stop to breathe.

The birds never get a chance, and have to go organize...form a disenfranchised victims support group, stage some kind of avian civil rights telethon, campaign for a federally-funded bird bail-out.

So, like any other spoiled brat who isn't getting his way, I hopped on the Internet to research ways to regain control of my bird feeder, to figure out how to modify Nature to make it fit *my* needs. And there it was:

Cayenne pepper.

Perfect. As it turns out, it's the capsaicin found in hot chiles that lands the punch. Squirrels hate it, but birds could care less about it. It was all explained to me on the Internet, by an online chemical repellent expert. Witness:

"According to [famous online chemical repellent expert], the ethmoid branch of the trigeminal nerve innervates the eyes, nose, and oral cavity. This is the nerve responsible for mediation of chemical irritation."

See? Could it be any obvious? Apparently, in the overarching scheme of things, birds are an ethmoid or so short. And as a famous television vixen might say, "It's a good thing."

So I blew a whole weekend spiking ten pounds of bird seed with ounce after ounce of ground red chiles. And believe me, you haven't lived till you've been stared at, standing in the grocery checkout line cradling sixty-five 2-ounce bottles of designer Cayenne Pepper.

And just in case you needed any further proof that the birds are gonna be okay, there's this from Famous Repellant Boy: "there is no evidence that birds code capsaicin as an irritant at concentrations as high as 20,000 ppm, but mammals like squirrels, rats, and mice reject capsicum concentrations as low as 1-10 ppm."

Hmmm. Maybe the brick-biting mice will eat the peppers, too. Then my fox will get to enjoy some Jalapeno poppers. (and I'm sure you saw *that* joke coming from about 20,000 ppm away)

See, it's all in the design. Reassuring, isn't it? This is all "big picture" stuff. It's all a part of Al Gore's plan.

And then I heard what I could've *sworn* was a Mariachi band.

I looked outside. And there, dangling upside-down from my bird feeder, were four squirrels wearing Haz-Mat masks and a poncho.

Involuntary Evolution

(Ever pondered the 'horse' part of 'horse pill?')

Well, it's a brand new year, and already I've learned something new. Understand - when you get to be my age, learning something new is Goal Number One. (Goal Number Two is remembering what you learned in Goal Number One.)

There's a Goal Number Three, too...I think. It has something to do with original sin, or not splitting infinitives, or bran.

I forget. That's just the way it goes. At my age, it's just a matter of time before I repeat something I just said, or forget what I wanted to say, or repeat something I just said.

So sometimes I forget. Leave me alone. I'm not an elephant - I'm a camel (as you'll see in a minute).

Anyway, here's what I learned this year, so far: the true definition of the word 'generic.' See, till now, I'd always thought 'generic' meant 'bland,' or it meant 'undistinguished,' or it meant you'd wasted the last half-hour at a party talking to someone researching their thesis on 'Hidden Old Testament References To Ellen DeGeneres.'

Nope. As it turns out, 'generic' -- in the medical profession, at least -- means 'theoretically affordable medication, if it actually existed in this galaxy, which it doesn't.' And 'non-generic' means 'laughably expensive, for no apparent reason.' Non-generic: kind of a synonym for the Department of Energy, really.

And here's how I came to this new-found knowledge. Late last year, at the tailing end of my nineteenth yearly physical, I sat shivering in the doctors' examining room, looking longingly across the room at my street clothes and reflexively massaging a cotton ball. During the previous hour-and-a-half, I had been duly weighed, splayed, pricked, prodded, dabbed, daubed and bled by a steady procession of future physicians, all wearing Dansko clogs and disposable scrub suits saturated with Scooby-Doo characters.

After the appropriate hope-sucking delay ... in whatever way that delay is calculated by the Union of Medical Practice Appointment-Overbooking Agents ... there came a tap on the door, a whoosh of air, and my doctor dashed in to the examining room, wearing open-toed soiree stilettos, a foul-weather jacket, and gripping a three-barbed marlin lure between her teeth.

As it turned out, I was her last hurdle before she navigated out the Cheyenne Mountain-like "Doctors Only" door to take several well-deserved weeks off, and make a boat payment. Apparently, she'd been steadily segueing into her civilian clothes, one examining room at a time, self-prepping for a dash to the marina.

As she blasted in, I felt a bit under-dressed, given that I was wearing nothing but an over-laundered paper gown and a cotton ball pressed against my ring finger, though I took comfort in knowing that, if I sprinted fast enough, I was mere seconds away from sporting both socks.

But on this day, Doctor Armada had no time for prurience, nor proprieties.

The doc cut straight to the chase. Consulting a chart, she told me she didn't like one of my 'numbers.' She stared at me in an accusing tone of voice, which was pretty sobering, given that I was nearly naked and she was chewing on a honed marlin spike. In the spirit of cooperative fellowship, I scoffed at my numbers and offered to pick a different number, if she'd just let me know which number had fallen out of favor.

But Doc Bimini was already scribbling prescriptions, or maybe a maritime-meal shopping list, and I don't think she heard me.

(To be honest, I had more at stake than simple cooperation -- I wanted to get out of there before the Scooby-Doo squad came back for more blood samples. They'd already hit me up for so much plasma that I no longer cast a reflection in the mirror.)

Then my doctor let me in on a little "inside baseball" news: the prescription drug I'd been taking for several years had been recalled. It seems that the drug company had released some recent research, revealing that taking this particular drug, at this particular dosage, could have "undesirable" consequences.

"Undesirable?" I squirmed.

Recent studies, she explained, showed that some test subjects had developed mildly discomforting symptoms, including headaches, something quite foul that involved the word "leakage," and a sudden manifestation of camel hooves.

I took issue. I pointed out that getting cloven feet is *not* what normal people would consider "undesirable." Wouldn't you agree? I mean, gassing up your car in the rain is undesirable. Getting an over-cooked fried egg - *that's* undesirable.

But turning part-way into a leaking dromedary with migraines goes *way* past "undesirable."

I don't think she heard me.

"We're going to change prescriptions," she announced.

"We?" I thought. "What's with this *'we?'* What're you now, my partner?"

"Keep in mind," she went on, avoiding my eyes. "This one isn't generic."

"Hey, Doc," I wondered aloud, "since *'we'* are going to switch prescriptions, and *'we'* are switching to brand-name drugs, that means *'we'* are going to split the brand-name cost, right? *Right?"*

Silence. No reply.

I don't think she heard me.

So I did what any self-respecting, virile, nearly naked, totally ignored American male would do when in the presence of a wildly successful female authority figure who owns a boat.

I ran away.

With all the hunter-gatherer manliness passed along by my forebears, I tactically positioned the cotton ball and reached for my socks.

Not that it mattered. My allotted time had expired, and the good doctor had to leave if she was going to float her boat before low tide.

On her way out, she told me to make appointments three times a month for my yearly physical, handed me a prescription form filled out in something, possibly Sanskrit, and reminded me to be sure and floss my hooves.

"Don't you mean *'our'* hooves, Nemo?"

We don't think she heard us.

I tossed my shredded left sock in the bin, grabbed the mate sock and, scowling at the hoof, silently vowed to be more careful with this one.

And on my way out, I stopped by the water cooler to fill up my hump.

I'm Just Sayin'

(Nothing special, this. Just sweeping clutter off the porch in my head.)

- I started reading a scientific article, warning that Facebook was creating a self-obsessed generation, but after two whole paragraphs, the article hadn't mentioned me, so I deleted it.

- The 614 Republican presidential candidates met in Iowa for a debate. In honor of the event, I ordered a tepid pizza with no ingredients or spices, watched as each slice ate each other, and then sent the bill to somebody else's grandchildren.

- A new drug claims to endow mice with 50% more stamina. Imagine the thesis underlying that research grant. Inside this lab, I'm guessing, is a clutch of undergrad interns who often call in sick.

- Women shoppers in Fairfax, Virginia reported there's some sick freak on the loose, who sneaks up behind them in malls and slashes their clothes. Local police are rounding up members of Congress for questioning.

- Some supermodel is suing some ex-somebody for over $40,000 a month in child support. Heck, I'd give her ten bucks just to watch the kid eat.

- I saw a guy on TV wearing a shirt with small checks, a jacket with large checks, and a polka-dot tie. And he wasn't even healing people!

- "If you experience persistent bleeding, contact your doctor." I did not need to be told that.

- This first-time-ever credit downgrade for the United States is not gonna go well. Saturday night, I called out for some Chinese takeaway. They demanded I bring THEM food.

- Barry's Posting Postulate: The credibility of an email's content is inversely proportional to the size of the font used in the email.

- Last week, at a birthday party in Chicago, Nancy Pelosi put on a Marilyn Monroe wig, popped out of a cake and started cooing "Happy Birthday, Mister President." The entire block had to be quarantined by the Center for Disease Control's roving Nausea Containment Squad.

- A cat food commercial is boasting "real ingredients." Pardon me? What other kind of ingredients are there?

- Only on Facebook can somebody ask for help harvesting a lucky Farmville leprechaun horoscope mafia hit cocktail biscuit coupon, and then turn around and challenge somebody else for making an ignorant comment.

- You can now buy a Shirley Temple DVD collection. Eighteen chronically cute Shirley Temple films. Think about that. Somewhere, right now, some family could be queuing up eighteen back-to-back Shirley Temple movies. I'd snap like a twig.

- Following on the heels of their wildly popular financial downgrade of the entire United States of America, Standard & Poor's finally got around to downgrading Fannie Mae and Freddie Mac, the Weimar Republic, and the 1637 Dutch Tulip Mania. On a roll, they then signaled a promising future for an exciting new drug they've been reading about, known as penicillin. Next week, according to an insider tip, they plan to announce the pending breakup of The Beatles.

- Casey Anthony is now kiting checks. What is it with this Ma Barker Redux? Is she packing some kind of Cosmic Get-Out-Of-Jail-Free card? If I miss a utilities payment by six hours, somebody downtown flips a switch, and suddenly I can't open my garage door.

- According to unnamed sources, Treasury Secretary Geithner "curses like a 7th-grade boy." So whatever happens with his iffy Treasury gig, Geithner'll be fine -- after all, with a mouth like that, he's a shoo-in for Vice President.

- I was thinking about forming a community group: Ignorant Southern Bigot Bomb-Throwing Reactionary White Vampire Racist Tea Party Terrorists, but I couldn't fit the ISBBTRWVRTPT logo on the guest towels at the lodge.

- That weird 12-member Super-Congressional-Committee of the Justice League All-Stars has finally been selected.

One of the chosen twelve is from my home state of South Carolina. Another of them, Senator John "Heinz 57 Opinions" Kerry, went on record to point out that he was from South Carolina before he wasn't.

- These medicine commercials (with their "mild, rare" side-effects) are getting ridiculous. "A small number of heart attacks, strokes, and heart-related deaths have been experienced while taking Thiskudenditol. Other symptoms may include stabbing ear pains, blindness, barking like a doomed slavering ex-pet in a Stephen King novel, and a staggering sense of having made a really bad decision."

- Earlier this week, madness reigned at a rally in Ohio, when bomb-throwing, hostage-taking, bigot vampire Tea Party members allowed a non-public-sector-union fetus to come to full term. The unholy mob (read: "voters") then invaded a retirement home, where they overturned an all-organic salad bar and made several rude "Soylent Green" jokes. Afterwards, they shape-shifted into bats, desecrated a copy of Charles Darwin's eighth-grade math test, and sacrificed a middle-class goat.

- Shortly after concluding their Discontinued Shuttle Parts yard sale, NASA launched an exploratory rocket to Jupiter. Their mission: ask around on Jupiter, see if anybody THERE has a cogent fiscal policy.

On a personal note, I'm just glad NASA picked Jupiter. Given the conditions in Congress, if they'd pursued funding for Uranus, the jokes could've kept me awake all night...

Wow! Nice Uvea!

(We all do it, we all hate it. No, not flossing.)

I couldn't believe it. Had a whole year really passed? Really? But there it was – the appointment card from my eye doctor's, which brooked no argument. It was time for my annual eyeball tune-up and lube.

End of discussion. Facts are facts, unless you're a pathological liar, or in politics. (Yeah, I know.)
You know the drill. And you know you have to do it. Even if *you* think your eyes are fine, you know you have to go. Even if you never mistake your mom for your dad. Even if once, last month, you went a whole day without running into things. You have to honor the eye doctor's appointment card.

And you get no points at all for being able to actually *read* the appointment card.

You know the drill. Every year, you have to put aside a couple of hours to get your eyes checked out by a professional Eye

Checker-Outer. They don't actually *say* "Eye Checker-Outer," of course. But for some unexplained reason, this branch of the medical profession couldn't settle for normal medical profession titles, like Dentist, or Pediatrician, or Demon Barber. So they putzed around with a Latin version of Boggle until they had enough syllables to call themselves Ophthalmologists (literal translation: Opthal Checker-Outer).

Step one, of course, once you arrive at the Opthalicron, is to peer through the little sliding-glass window at an empty check-in desk. Eventually, someone will drift past the desk, possibly by mistake, and immediately not notice you (maybe they should go get *their* eyes checked). After some undefined period of time, the lady (it's always a lady), who's wearing some kind of loose-fitting outfit stamped with Flintstones cartoon characters (it's always either the Flintstones or Scooby-Doo), will not look directly at you and ask you if your insurance has changed.

Your insurance status is what defines what will happen, or won't happen, next. Your insurance status is more important than incidental trivia like your name, how your kids are doing in school, or the fact that you're bleeding freely from the forehead and holding your detached left leg in your right arm.

It doesn't help matters, either, that Flintstone Lady always seems just a tiny bit bitter (perhaps due to having made a career choice that involves going to lunch five days a week with other ladies, all wearing loose-fitting Flintstone pajamas).

Anyway, after you've scribbled through the formalities, Flintstone Lady ushers you into the examining chamber, a dimly-lit windowless room inevitably decorated, like all medical and dental facilities, in a neutral-colors theme so foul that you can actually buy it at Home Depot, should you have such an aberrant urge (just ask for Early Appalachian Orthodontia). This color scheme is the result of years of secret CIA research in psychological warfare, designed to turn the targeted human into a pliant dweeb who will numbly accept commands like "Yes, everything but your underwear" and "Okay, now spit."

There's something about that chair in the eye doctor's examining room that makes the visitor feel like an undersized space alien, about to be questioned or … gulp … probed. You're sitting there in the semi-darkness, surrounded by lots of looming, off-white machinery, as if you'd been kidnapped and spirited off to some sort of evil Swivel Museum.

After tapping a computer keyboard for a while, Flintstone Lady felt her way over to my ecto-chair and, with no explanation whatsoever, handed me a preparatory Kleenex. She began to manipulate the machine's eerily organic elements, all of which required me to "rest your chin here," a phrase I haven't heard since watching a very dismal Lifetime Channel mini-series about the French Revolution.

For a while, we played some kind of weird game where she Gatling-gunned slides at me and kept yelling, "Better? Or worse?"

I never did find out my score.

Finally, Flintstone Lady zapped me with a three-gallon dose of eye drops, turned on a little projector, and made me read very tiny, incredibly misspelled words.

This is it? This is the pinnacle of progress in medical science? You're sitting in a dark closet with a mildly bitter adult. Your eyes are dripping some kind of eye-drop residue the consistency of queso and the color of three-week-old sun-dried ferret. And you're being forced to recite words like "LZ3VRTSX" to a professional wearing pajamas.

By the time Flintstone Lady's silhouette made her exit, my eyes looked like an Audrey Hepburn movie poster. I was so dilated I was afraid I might go into labor.

In spite of it all, though, going to the eye doctor's office beats going to the "full-body-contact" doctor's office in three important ways. Firstly, you don't have to get weighed. Secondly, you don't have to take off all your clothes, put on a gown that would show off your cleavage if your cleavage was on your back, and sit, shivering, on a roll of generic gift-wrapping paper.

The other advantage of visiting the eye doctor's is a conspicuous absence of specimen cups. If you're ever at an eye doctor's office, and any Scooby-Doo'd staffer hands you a specimen cup, you should demand to see some ID. Or just tell them you have no insurance.

Finally, the doctor himself, the actual Optimal Thologist, decided to drop by. He asked how my insurance was doing; had I experienced any blurred vision; had I noticed any running into poles and nearby people.

I did get some good news, though. I think. I'm not sure, because by this point the eye drops were puddling in my ears, but I think the eye doc said I might get an early Cadillac.

Then he handed me a bill for the Kleenex, opened the closet door, and disappeared into a halo of light.

Minutes passed. Machinery hummed. A speaker in the ceiling looped through bad orchestral arrangements of Neil Diamond tunes, but I was too dilated to escape. In my mind, I began to organize my last will and testament. I calmed my soul.

Not to worry. Flintstone Lady finally re-materialized and outfitted me with an embarrassingly cheesy dark-glasses device – a temporary, die-cut piece of light-defying plastic that was supposed to cling to my glasses and protect my poor, dilated eyeballs from sunlight, as long as I avoided sunlight.

The faux glasses did *not* deliver – I merely transitioned from living in a blurred world to living in a blurred, dark world. All the glasses accomplished was to make shield my face while cursing at daylight, while simultaneously making me look like Will Smith playing Ray Charles, but less rich.

I couldn't focus, I certainly couldn't drive, and I was behaving like Will Smith playing Helen Keller, but less cute. So, for the rest of morning, I sat on a bench outside the office, holding a specimen cup and singing the blues.

Not a bad morning, as it turned out. I pulled down twenty-eight bucks.

That'll almost cover the Kleenex.

Living to Death, Part 3

(The high cost of free health care)

Not long ago, I told you about my doctor's insistence that I get yearly checkups weekly, in order to ensure my ability to keep having health, and her ability to keep making boat payments.

I also told you about her directive for me to switch to a 'non-generic' drug. I didn't think much about it at the time, though I do remember noticing that, during the whole 'non-generic' discussion, she refused to look me in the eye. It gave me that same nervous feeling you get at a used-car lot after pointing out some weird stains on the dashboard, causing the used-car salesman to nonchalantly mention the car's low mileage, due to the previous owner's recent incarceration in a maximum security compound for the criminally insane.

But I never finished the story. Because I couldn't. I literally, physically couldn't. For several weeks after the 'non-generic' episode, every time I'd think back on it, I'd black out.

Therefore, my therapist insists, I need to face the fear. I need to get the story out, lest I morph into some rage-filled fiend with a suspiciously shrinking collection of friends, and odd dashboard stains.

Now, normally, my monthly visits to the pharmacy are a quick in-and-out.

Me: Hi, I called in a prescription refill.
White Lab Coat Person: Do you have your Super-Saver Drastic-Discount Big-Bonus-Bucks preferred customer card?
Me: I didn't think the card applied to prescriptions.
Lab Coat: It doesn't.
Me: Pardon me for a minute. I need to black out.

But this time, I had this new 'non-generic' prescription to fill. I'd brought the little tear-off sheet they gave me at the doctor's, imprinted with their office location and phone, and bearing what was either my doctor's handwriting or some kind of ink-based performance art. On faith alone, I assumed the unintelligible scribble was my prescription, though, for all I knew, it could have been an equation challenging special relativity, the Pentagon's nuclear launch codes, or a line drawing of a hysterectomy performed during a hurricane.

Me: Hi, I have this new prescription to fill.
Lab Coat: Do you have your Super-Saver Drastic-Discount Big-Bonus-Bucks preferred customer card?
Me: Fine, thanks. How are you?
Lab Coat: Do you have your Super-Saver Drastic-Discount Big-Bonus-Bucks preferred customer card?

Me: I do. But enough about me - let's talk about *you* for a while!

Lab Coat: May I see your little tear-off sheet?

Me: Well, okay. But at this point I still think we should see other people.

Lab Coat: Sir, this prescription is for a non-generic drug!

Me: Yeah, that's what my doct ... Hey! Why did you stop looking me in the eye?

Then came the revelation. Lab Coat Person tapped for a bit on his computer screen, then spun the screen round, averted his eyes, and showed me the price of my new, 'non-generic' prescription.

Whoa.

Some drug company somewhere is awfully proud of that little pill.

I thought there was some mistake. I thought maybe Lab Coat had mistakenly googled census statistics, or the Greek debt. I couldn't get my head around it. I didn't want to *marry* the little pill; I just wanted to occasionally ingest the thing. Was I filling a scrip or funding a Spielberg epic? Was I buying a month's supply of pills or a member of Congress?

Turns out this drug is so expensive, my neighborhood pharmacy doesn't even bother stocking it. People in my income bracket don't rate that level of health care. Demographically speaking, nobody that lives near me can afford to get *that* well.

It looked like I would have to go to some other pharmacy. No big deal, that. When it comes to city planning, my neighborhood follows the plan of every other neighborhood in the American South. At any given four-way intersection in the South, if there's a traffic light, the real estate layout is the same:

Corner 1: a pharmacy
Corner 2: a different pharmacy
Corner 3: a Spinx gas station
Corner 4: a Baptist church

(Very few laymen realize the integral role that intersections have played in the growth of the Baptist church in the South. Without corners, we might all be Lutherans. And that would be the end of NASCAR as we know it.)

So I had a decision to make: I could walk across the street to the competitor's pharmacy (Soylent WalGreen) and fill out "new customer" paperwork for about eleven weeks, or I could drive to the next nearest "sister" store of my own pharmacy, which, thanks to the Baptist Intersection Theory, was a trek of almost two whole blocks. Suddenly, Lab Coat closed the deal by offering to call the sister store for me, if I promised not to tell anybody that he'd shattered protocol by actually assisting me *before* I presented my Super-Saver card.

What a selfless gesture! I'll admit - it touched me. But then, I'm in monthly therapy twice a week.

Despite being located in a much tonier neighborhood, the sister pharmacy was a clone of my own...for the most part. But there were some subtle differences. For instance, this pharmacy stored the cartons of cigarettes just *below* the boxes of nicotine patches, rather than just above.

This upscale druggist's had *six* cash registers with only one register open, as opposed to the 3/1 configuration at my usual haunt. (Both pharmacies, however, still had just the one on-duty teenage clerk with face piercings.)

There at La Pharmatique, they barely let you through the accordion doors before bombarding you with the gauntlet of garish magazines dedicated to celebrity stupidities and female insecurities. One front cover's screaming headline managed to tease to both audiences: "Sex so good, you'll think you're with two-and-a-half men!"

Whatever. At my age, I don't need help having massive sex. At my age, I need help having matching socks.

The staff pharmacist there at Chez Drug was a very nice woman, who hailed from some country that doesn't have a future tense.

Lab Coat: You, I am welcoming! May I be helping you?
Me: Hi, here's my Super-Saver Drastic-Discount Big-Bonus-Bucks preferred customer card.
Lab Coat: Are you having your Super-Saver Drastic-Discount Big-Bonus-Bucks preferred customer card?
Me: Really? Seriously?
Lab Coat: I shall be waiting. I am being here all day.
Me: I drove over from your low-rent cousin pharmacy - you know, over there in the shady part of town, where we have open

sewers, closed minds, no feng shui, and we drink Cokes straight out of the can, without a straw.

Lab Coat: Yes, we are having your prescription filled already. Please be seating yourself for thirty minutes.

Me: Thirty minutes? But you said it's already filled!

Lab Coat: That is what you are getting for that 'future tense' crack, Mr. Smarty.

Touché. Big pharma karma.

And so, thirty-one minutes later, my staggeringly expensive pills and I drove home, where we eyeballed each other for a while, and then split a tuna fish sandwich. Later, I hit the streets to try and land a second job. When I left, the pills were curled up on the couch, watching a Jacqueline Susann film festival on *Lifetime*.

Well, there it is. That's the story, and my therapist was right - I *do* feel better. And I'm glad to get that behind me, before my two monthly therapy sessions this week.

After all, therapists have boat payments, too.

Noir, Y'all

(An unfinished chapter from a non-existent novel)

It was a dark and nightly storm.

An improbable moon scudded across an unwilling canvas of really dark sky, invoking the deployment of some seriously obscure "dark" synonym, possibly even ebon.

Me, I was working late at the office, trying to make some sense out of this latest puzzler, and getting nowhere slowly. (A three-letter word for 'salamander?' Are they kiddin'? What happened to 'newt?') Outside, beyond the greased grease that scudded against the window of my second-story walkup, rain thundered like lightning. Across the scudded hall, I could hear Mary McMary cackling as she reeled in one jaded, hopeless, burned-out cell phone subscriber after another. And still no word from my rent ticket ... my latest client, Howland Payne ... about his missing hypnotist.

Another day in Paradise.

In the gutter across the two-lane blackened moist-top, I could still see the dwarf. He was eating another eraser. He makes for a sad tale, this palooka, and he's too far gone to listen to reason. Sad. Just another eraser junkie. Not long ago, this was the strapping, six-foot-four bouncer down at Geronimo's, and life was laid out before him like a life buffet might be laid out, if parts of life came in bowls or steam trays and needed a sneeze guard. Another metaphor I could use might be, oh, a buffet of life-parts, if such things were all part of a full life, or part of a healthy breakfast.

But the dwarf's too far gone. The erasers are winning. At this rate, he'll wipe himself out before his next monthly stimulus check arrives.

But I was still alive. My luck was holding. Yeah, that's right. My luck is normally as rotten as a thing that reminds you of some luck-based thing that might rot, but lately it was holding, like a thing might hold if it got itself compared to rotten luck in one of those mood-setting "pattern of rottenness" descriptions you find in the early-on exposition of these types of stories. As it were.

Stick around. I have more similes.

The luck of a free-lance crossword detective often gets taken for granted, especially by all those get-rich-quick formulaic writers in the best-seller lists, all those imperfect caricature artists who just don't appreciate a real brush with death. Got to have that large spool of luck steadily threading the bobbin of your life (unless I mean treadle, or maybe feed dogs), or you end up just one more splotch on the side of the road, a cold memory, a scudding speck of tepid mold, a pitiful, unwanted, used-up, shot-down, empty shell of a man whose life remains unfulfilled without that elusive three-letter salamander synonym.

Enough introspection. Time for a break. I'm getting a headache; plus, some of my upcoming similes require me to segue into the present tense. I sweep keys and crossword from my tarnished (tainted, tawdry, tallow-stained, turn-of-the-century) desk, grab my hat and coat, and pocket my gat (my gun, my rod, my heater, my widow-maker, my argument ender, my little overdue-library-book equalizer). Out the door and two blocks east, down to the corner of Thirteenth and Lesion, to toss back a few quick ones at Geronimo's place.

As I begin to step inside, I'm nearly Vienna Boys Choir-ed by an outbound umbrella, wielded by a diminutive but stunning Asian woman, storming through me and into the scudding rainstorm. I side-step the self-absorbed petite patron and ease onto a corner stool. Geronimo nods. I nod. He raises one eyebrow and two fingers. I nod again.

Transaction completed.

"Nice stems," I open, arching my head toward the exiting Asian.

"She'll eat your face," Geronimo castles and counters. Checkmate.

A shot glass and unlabeled bottle glide (or possibly scud) to a stop within my reach. I review the label and sniff the cork, or I would have, if I had paid just a *little* more attention in school, so that I could have ended up in a different kind of story than this one.

Suddenly, another problem. I smell them before I see them. The twins. The Enoff boys, Buzz and Bob, who recently resurfaced after spending ten long at County due to my testimony, and who seem to have taken the whole event a bit personally. They've pulled up to the curb outside, more or less seated on a brace of dead-silent, green-friendly, all-electric highway bikes.

My luck holds. The Enoff brothers waddle blindly into Geronimo's, their Idaho-sized heads locked backwards, waxing priapic, watching the south end of that sultry northbound Asian. They don't see me.

Embracing a nearby metaphor, I grab at the proverbial brass ring and manage to oil into the nearest faux naugahyde booth, subtly arranging the soiled tablecloth around my head like a Hindu turban. The confused couple who were already occupying the booth take a few seconds to regroup, probably weighing candidates from among their list of possible greetings. I grin menacingly, touch my turban, slip them a fiver, and make what may or may not have been a kindly but stern Hindi hand gesture. The young couple prove to be a quick study - the woman winks, dabs ashes on her forehead and molds her fingers in an elegant pranam mudra. Her date faints.

Geronimo, scanning the scenario, reacts. "Uh, just missed him again, boys," he grins. So now I owe him, too. Obviously, dead presidents are gonna flutter tonight.

290

As clever as ever, the Enoff boys realize Geronimo is speaking to them. Awareness spins the twins, and they stare at the bartender. "Oh, yeah?" quips Bob Enoff, leaping into the lead in this literary le Mans.

Geronimo, eyelid twitching, begins to wipe down the bar. He flicks a short eye at me and leans into diversion. "Close game last week, huh?" he skats, automatically mixing up a couple of Wrangler Wildcats.

(Great. Another fiver.)

Buzz Enoff sneers and attacks a defenseless bar stool. His fingers ruthlessly pinch the offered shot glass, his nostrils flare, he slaps glass to lips, he slurps, he blanches, he belches. He speaks.

"...urp."

Class will tell.

Bob Enoff reaches in his pocket and pulls out a glittering, clinking something and tosses it on the bar. "Found these out front, cocky. Look familiar?" I hear the thing slide across the bar. Geronimo says nothing.

I make eye contact with the girl at my table. "What's he got, and what's your name?" I whisper, as I slowly push her still non-functional date down to the floor.

"Looks like some car keys," mouths the pleasantly attractive girl. "Ophelia. Nice to meet you."

Ophelia smiles and my headache returns. A low moan drifts up from underneath the table.

"Is that a pistol in your pocket or are you just gl..."

"Knock it off, Ophelia," I mumble. I pull back the edge of my turban and make a micro-turn toward the bar. Geronimo is holding a Saab key ring, three keys swaying back and forth. For some reason, I wonder, again, what happened to that hypnotist.

"Can't help you there, guys," Geronimo declares, "but I'll hang on to 'em. Somebody'll claim 'em."

Buzz sniffs and rubs a paw across his mouth. "Gimme them keys back, cocky," he glares. "I think I know who they belong."

Coolly, Geronimo keeps swinging the keys, slowly and steadily, in a precise rhythm, a ... hypnotic ... rhythm. When he speaks, his voice sounds different.

"--- Wouldn't you rather --- I keep them --- wouldn't you rather --- leave them --- with me --- while you --- go tell the Fat Man --- his accountant --- forgot the car keys ---"

The twins are transfixed. I am amazed. Ophelia rubs her eyes. Her date moans. I put my foot in his mouth. Geronimo slowly lowers the keys to the bar.

"Bye-bye, boys," he intones.

Buzz and Bob Enoff rise like lumpy puppets, turn away, and lumber oddly, metrically out into the night.

When the door closes behind them, I jump up, peck Ophelia on the cheek, shove my turban in her date's mouth, and leap scuddingly to the bar.

"Where the heck did you learn that?"

Geronimo smiles and pours a couple shots. He nails one and hands me the other. "You pick up a lot of tricks in this trade," he says. "Payne's hypnotist was a little short of ready cash once, and we ... worked something out."

"Impressive," I reply, "very impressive. Useful. Utile. Convenient. Expedient. Handy. Hey, you don't happen to know a three-letter word for 'salamander,' do ya?"

Geronimo looks at me closely, as if I might suddenly start biting things.

"Eft."

"Thanks, G. Hey, wait a minute. You said 'the accountant forgot the car keys.' *What* accountant forgot the car keys?"

"That accountant," Geronimo responds, pointing behind me. I turn to look and see nothing. Well, nothing but Ophelia winking at me, which does nothing to help my headache.

"Geronimo," I ask, "you don't mean that illegal-in-several-states little dumpling is an accountant, do you?"

"No," he says, "but her date, the prone guy presently gargling with my tablecloth, is."

Hmm, I think. No wonder he fainted. A total stranger handing an accountant five bucks.

I start to pursue this twist when I feel something at my side. Turning, I see Ophelia, chest flashing, eyes heaving, pressing a business card into my palm. "Call me," she breathes. "We should talk."

I look at the card: Pinner & Lever Confectioners -- Ophelia Payne, Junior Icer.

PAYNE!?!

(Stay tuned for next week's episode! Though probably not!)

Duck! Soup!

(When healthy food kills you, who do you call?)

This week, I made a fascinating culinary discovery, which I'll share with you here, absolutely free. Got a pen ready? Okay. If you violently shake a can of Campbell's soup before cooking, you may find that it can slip from your grasp and then imitate a Wile E. Coyote-style kitchen wall-penetrating missile.

I may be the only person on Earth who, while innocently transporting something as NATO-neutral as a border-agnostic tin of tame tomato soup, could be warned, "Careful! You could put somebody's eye out!"

Leave it to me to go ballistic with broth.

And trust me - when a high-speed can of hearty vegetables impacts with innocent sheetrock, what a sound it makes! It sounds a lot like a footfall from that rogue *Jurassic Park* T-Rex, pursuing a J-Park jeep and about to lay into a can of condensed Jeff Goldblum, but with more sodium.

So now I need to find a handyman - some skilled expert who can de-Campbell-ize my dented kitchen wall. And that presents a new challenge. Among the many things that I don't do well (repairing drywall, respecting authority, holding on to food), I always seem to have a hard time actually *finding* a company or service's phone number in the phone book. Specifically, in those irritating yellowed pages.

The white pages are a snap, as long as you know more about the person you need to call than just 'Bob.' Personally, I can only remember the last names of about eight people, and six of *those* people are in my immediate family.

And forget the blue pages. Only the government would list a City Manager, *and* an Assistant City Manager, *and* a Deputy Assistant City Manager, and then show them all as having the same phone number. And after you learn that your tax dollars are paying for some government drone with the job title 'Adjutant Assisting Pro-Tem Secretary to the Assistant Sitting Under-Secretary to the As-Yet Unindicted East Coast Director for Post-Menopausal Shrimp Stress Research Grants,' you're too depressed to bother calling anybody anyway.

On the other hand, the canary-colored pages were designed *specifically* to make it easy to find stuff. Weren't they? The phone company is our friend, right? That's what I was always taught as a child, anyway, back at Ma Bell High School, and every summer at Telecom Monopoly Employee's Union Vacation Bible School.

But the lemon page listings *don't* help: they only confuse the issue. Sure, there are the eye-poppingly obvious listings: Welding (see also *Metalworking*). Zippers. Cabinetry (see also *Kitchens* and *Caskets*). Small Caliber Ammunition. Fish Bait. All the things your average guy needs, if your average guy is involved in Chicago politics and is going to spend the weekend 'cleaning up some loose ends.'

Anything more complex, though, and the trouble begins. Because the phone company's Category Team refuses to call anything by the same name that *we* use here on Earth. I can never guess what term *they're* using to point at the term *I'm* using.

You know what I mean: Let's say you need your grass cut. So what you need is the phone number of some bipedal mammal who can parse the straightforward sentence, "If you will cut my grass, I will pay you." Granted, in addition to being able to walk upright and read single syllable words, you would also prefer somebody who's unindicted, who's been in the country more than 20 days, and who still has a few of their original teeth (though, to be fair, that's more than we expect from sitting members of Congress).

So, being a clever citizen, you thumb-rifle through the Jaundice Pages to the C's (for 'cut'). Nothing. On, then, to the G's (for 'grass'). Nothing. On a whim, you think 'Lawnmower Man' and try the S's (for 'very weird Stephen King short story that was the victim of possibly the worst movie adaptation of all time'). Nada. Zip. Bupkis.

(Because you weren't paying attention at school, you don't think to try 'peat' or 'sod.' Not that it would've mattered.)

See, the Banana Book calls that particular activity 'Lawn Maintenance' or 'Landscaping' (see also *Lawn Maintenance*) or 'Modular Waterfall Gardens That Double As Mosquito Breeding Farms.' At least, that what's they call it *today*. Next week, try looking up 'Landscaping' and you'll get nothing but a cross-reference that says 'see also *Unemployed Beach-Front Property Realtors That Now Cut Grass*.' Well, that and a giant refrigerator magnet from a legal firm, just dropping by to check on your health. ("*Ever been hurt by a waterfall garden? Ever been pregnant? Ever taken Cantsleepital? Ever known anyone who was taking Cantsleepital while standing near a pregnant waterfall garden? Ever spelled 'asbestos' correctly? If so, you may be entitled to millions of dollars in settlement claims of which, after our fees and costs, you will get to keep about seventy-five cents! Call 'We Are Legion' Legal Services today!*")

So the upshot is you just can't easily use the Butter-Colored Pages to find something as commonplace as lawn mowing. On the other hand, if you're staring helplessly at a flat coil (whatever *that* is), and are desperately in need of someone who can 'distr' it (whatever *that* is), you can riffle right to a category called 'Springs-Coil, Flat, Etc. Distrs & Mfrs.' (What a 'distr' is, I don't know. And based on what passes as acceptable on TV sitcoms these days, what a 'mfr' is short for, I don't *want* to know.)

Besides, it seems to me that 'flat coil' is an oxymoron. It's either coiled, or it's flat. And if you're looking for tactical help to deal with a straight piece of flat wire, well, maybe you have bigger issues than finding the right distr for your (ex)coil. It's like the thinking behind having a listing for 'Breast-Feeding Coordinator.' I mean, I ask you - how dumb do you have to be to need someone to swing round and coordinate your breast-feeding?

Imagine, if you will, Day Five at Toni's School of Future Beauticians & Breast-Feeding Coordinators.
Instructor: "Very good, class! Next week ... the other one!"

And then there's all that 'see also' phone book clutter. To be fair, I'm sure that the Ochre Gourd Pages had the best of intentions when they came up with the 'see also' concept. But their implementation of the concept leaves a lot to be desired, kind of like the European Union, or microwaveable pork. For example, category 'Floor Waxing' recommends you 'see also *Floor Laying*.'

Sorry. That's just a flawed analogy. Waxing and Laying? That's not even close, as any self-respecting hen will tell you.

Why not some seriously useful cross-referencing?

- College Athletics (see also *Professional Athletics*)
- Chicago Politics (see also *Lake Michigan* and *Sonar, Retail*)
- Catholic Churches (see also *Sins, Carnal* and *Sins, Venal*)
- Poultry Discipline (see also *Hen Waxing*)
- Doughnuts, Wholesale (see also *Men's Plus-Sized Jeans*)
- 'Die Hard' Sequels (see also *Enough Already*)
- Baptist Churches, Southern (see also *Potato Salad Recipes*)
- Cantsleepital, Retail, (don't see also *Heavy Machinery*)
- Cantsleepital, Potentially Fatal Side-Effects (see also *Giant Refrigerator Magnets, Obnoxious*)

- Predestination Services (foresee also *Presbyterian Churches*)
- Nagging Wife, Persistent (see also *Diamonds, Retail*)
- Hot Dogs, Total Enlightenment (see also *Make Me One With Everything*)
- Hope (see also *Change*)
- Jury Tampering, Wholesale (see also *Chicago Politics*)

And sometimes, cross-referencing just fails. Just. Simply. Fails. Here's an example: in the Summer Squash-colored pages of a nearby phone book that I borrowed (see also *stole*), I noticed this handy listing - and I am not making this up:

Fish Ponds (see also *Fish Ponds*).

On the other hand, 'Chimney Lining Materials' was listed just next to 'Chinese Food Products.'

Hmm. Maybe these guys are smarter than I thought.

About the Author

Barry Parham is a recovering software freelancer and the author of humor columns, essays and short stories. He is a music fanatic and a 1981 honors graduate of the University of Georgia.

Writing awards and recognitions earned by Parham include taking First Place in the November 2009 Writer's Circle Competition, First Prize in the March 2012 writing contest at HumorPress.com, and a plug by the official website of the Erma Bombeck Writers' Workshop. His work also appeared in the 2011 national humor anthology, *My Funny Valentine*.

Author's website
http://www.pmwebs.com

@ Facebook
http://www.facebook.com/profile.php?id=1114641029

@ Twitter
http://twitter.com/barryparham

Made in the USA
Charleston, SC
30 April 2012